10

The Alarming History of Sex

RICHARD GORDON

The Alarming History of Sex

106Sex and All That

For Bart's

Richard Gordon

1996

SINCLAIR-STEVENSON

5/8/96
M

First published in Great Britain in 1996
by Sinclair-Stevenson
an imprint of Reed International Books Ltd
Michelin House, 81 Fulham Road, London sw3 6rb
and Auckland, Melbourne, Singapore and Toronto

A CIP catalogue record for this book
is available at the British Library
isbn 1 85619 493 0

Phototypeset in Linotron Trump Medieval 11/13½pt
by Intype London Ltd
Printed and bound in Great Britain
by Clays Ltd, St Ives plc

Yes, this was love, this ridiculous bouncing of the buttocks,
and the wilting of the poor, insignificant, moist little
penis. This was the divine love! After all, the moderns were
right when they felt contempt for the performance; for it
was a performance. It was quite true, as some poets said,
that the God who created man must have had a sinister
sense of humour, creating him a reasonable being, yet
forcing him to take this ridiculous posture, and driving
him with blind craving for this ridiculous performance.

D. H. Lawrence, Lady Chatterley's Lover

... the trivial and vulgar way of coition; it is the foolishest
act a wise man commits in all his life ...

Sir Thomas Browne, Religio Medici

The stage is more beholding to love than the life of man.
For as to the stage, love is ever a matter of comedies, and
now and then of tragedies: but in life it doth much mischief;
sometimes like a siren, sometimes like a fury.

Bacon, Of Love

And most of all would I flee from the cruel madness of love,
The honey of poison-flowers and all the measureless ill.

Tennyson, Maud

'. a Spartan servant girl,' said Pantagruel, 'when she was
asked whether she had ever had intercourse with a man,
she answered, "Never," but that occasionally men had had
intercourse with her.'

François Rabelais, Gargantua and Pantagruel

Someone asked Sophocles, 'How do you feel now about sex?
Are you still able to have a woman?' He replied, 'Hush, man;
most gladly indeed I am rid of it all, as though I had escaped
from a mad and savage master.'

Plato, Republic

It is an axiom that something is always happening between
a man and a woman, whether they're kissing or talking or
silently listening to music, even if it's only that they're
getting bored and moving apart.

Mervyn Jones, John and Mary

The education of all beautiful women is the knowledge of men.

F. Scott Fitzgerald, *This Side of Paradise*

A fool and his money are soon married.

Anon

A wise reviewer once said that there are too many books about sex, and the only way to reduce their number would be to make it mandatory for a full-frontal nude photograph of the author to appear on the dust-jacket.

Ronald Hyam, *Empire and Sexuality*

Contents

ONE

In the Beginning

. . . .

And God called the dry land Earth; and the gathering together
of the waters called he Seas: and God saw that it was good.

And God created great whales, and every living creature
that moveth, which the waters brought forth abundantly,
after their kind, and every winged fowl after his kind: and
God saw that it was good.

And God blessed them, saying, Be fruitful and multiply,
and fill the waters in the seas, and let fowl multiply in the
earth.

And God created man in his own image, in the image of
God created he him; male and female created he them.

And God blessed them, and God said unto them, Be fruitful
and multiply, and replenish the earth, and subdue it: and
have dominion over the fish of the sea, and over the fowl of
the air, and over every living thing that moveth upon the
earth.

And God saw every thing that he had made, and, behold,
it was very good. And the evening and the morning were
the sixth day

Genesis 1: 10, 21, 22, 27, 28, 31

. . . .

A Fable

God's in his heaven, all's right with the newfangled
world!

God sat heavily upon his throne, twitched his purple
mantle, wearily crossed his sandal-shod feet, reached for
an onyx beaker of nectar (supplied by the neighbouring

I

establishment on Olympus) and reflected gratefully that tomorrow was Sunday and his day off.

He ran his fingers through his long curly beard. The creatures great and small, which he had created in such a busy week, he had repeatedly enjoined to multiply. But would they?

The process was sublimely simple. In the lower creatures, the male's spermatazoa-producing organ was vaguely rubbed against the female's egg-deliverer. In the higher lot, this was performed more precisely by transient transformation of the penis into a syringe. But why, he reasoned, should the man bother, or even consider, putting this awkwardly elongated organ into a female's vagina? It was a clumsy manoeuvre, like sticking in an elbow to test the temperature of his bathwater. And why should a female, dutifully complying to multiply, first experience a personal affront equivalent to somebody rummaging in her handbag?

God extended his beaker to a cherub hovering with a golden amphora.

Perhaps he should re-jig the higher animals? he wondered. They could multiply less troublesomely by merely dividing into two, like the simple bacteria and protozoa which he had nonchalantly created, after the great whales, to express his versatility. But no. Identical men and identical women, when there were millions of them, would be uncompassionately boring, and unjust on the portrait painters. Sexual reproduction must be workable, like nourishment. Why did humans eat? Because they liked it. Right! They would multiply because they liked doing *that* far, far, far better than absolutely anything else which they could possibly ever want to do, or even think of doing! After the weekend he would summon his newly created man and effect an adjustment. He needed a gardener, anyway.

2

He tossed his beaker to a cherub and went for a shower in the water which he had created on Day One.

On Monday morning, God came purposefully to work. He happily surveyed the plants and herbs which he had created in the fields spread before him, then clapped his brow. He had forgotten to make rain. The magnificent crop would wilt and swiftly die of drought. He caused a thick mist to rise from the earth, and it poured.

God sat in the celestial window chewing ambrosia supplied by the Olympus Express Home Delivery. He grew bored, and made a few rainbows. Then he perceived in his wisdom that only a fool would employ a gardener without stringent references concerning his honesty, energy, sobriety, civility, lack of garrulity, freedom from autocracy and disinclination to take elevenses several times a morning. He decided it best to make his own. Once it stopped raining, God went out, gathered up some dust, gave it the kiss of life, and there he was.

When God next wandered into his delightful riverside garden at Eden, the naked gardener had his scythe propped against the apple tree, eating strawberries.

'Doubtless God could have made a better berry, but doubtless God never did,' said the gardener.

'Thank you. I'll get that quoted somewhere. You know you're not to touch the apples? They'd kill you. You haven't dead-headed the roses.'

'Look, God, I can't do everything,' the gardener grumbled. 'Not when you're growing here every tree that is pleasant to the sight, and good for food, you said as much yourself. I've only got one pair of hands.'

'Then I'll get you another pair.'

In anticipation of surgical handicraft, God administered an anaesthetic and deftly performed extrathoracic resection of the gardener's left twelfth rib. He closed the incision scarlessly with a subcuticular stitch and applied balm of Gilead. He turned the rib into a woman and

3

decided to call her Eve, because it went so well with Adam.

When God returned to enjoy the cool of the evening, he could not find them anywhere.

'Where art thou?' he called impatiently.

The pair were hidden in the bushes, copulating as joyously as his angels' quivering harp-strings.

'You've been eating those apples,' God said accusingly.

' 'Course we haven't,' Adam disagreed breathlessly.

'Thou shalt not bear false witness,' God thundered, creating lightning-flashes for emphasis.

'It was that serpent,' muttered Eve guiltily, sitting up. 'He said it would be all right. Where's my fig-leaf?'

God stared at her. What were those two huge rose-tipped bulges on her chest for? Ah! yes . . .

Sensing his thoughts, Adam protested: 'You told us to go forth and multiply.'

'Not in my garden,' God told him sharply.

'Where else can we go to, then?' Adam objected surlily, adjusting his fig-leaf.

God said: 'You're fired.'

Eve burst into tears. 'I like multiplying. It's lovely.'

'We don't give a fig,' Adam told God defiantly. 'We've got one another, that's enough.'

Adam and Eve clasped each other fiercely.

God was at a loss. 'You can go back to the land you came from,' he offered compassionately. 'Treat it like your own. You can till it, raise sheep and so on. Farmers are going to do pretty well. But please don't come back here,' he added sternly. 'I'll be putting an armed security man on the gate.'

God vanished, pausing to snap his fingers and transform the apples, into which he had concentrated all the aphrodisiac, narcotic, hallucinogenic and ecstatic qualities of his brave new world, into an innocuous and health-preserving fruit.

4

God sat over his cool evening goblet, deeply worried. Had he gone over the top with that certain feeling? Should it really be no more intense than the well-filled pleasure of finishing a steak and chips? The enthusiasm of Adam's and Eve's embrace had startled him. Multiplying clearly engendered a strong togetherness. They could not do it as casually as codfish.

He stroked his beard thoughtfully. But what if one of the duet tired of twanging the angelic music from the same old harp and reached for another? There would be unbearable disharmony. And what of its effects on the poor little products of his multiplication table?

Come to think of it, how would this overpowering feeling affect other activities of humans? Old Adams would certainly make silly asses of themselves over young Eves. God recalled – seeing the future as clearly as the past – that he would have James Thurber write in 1929: 'Woman, observing that her mate went out of his way to make himself entertaining, rightly surmised that sex had something to do with it. From that she logically concluded that sex was recreational rather than procreational.' The male would strain to attract the female by accumulating pieces of silver, by the composition of odes, by driving furiously a well-burnished chariot, while the female wasted her substance on seductive garments, once the fig-leaf became *démodé*.

You could not have everyone doing it everywhere with everyone, God reasoned sagaciously. Nobody would get to work. He reflected even more sombrely that multiplying invited the flagrant breaking not only of Commandments Nos. 7 and 10 (b), but of No. 9 frequently, and even of No. 6! Supposing Eve got paid for providing the lovely feeling, he speculated nervously, as she might for doing the cooking? Supposing Adam preferred Adams and Eve Eves? Heavens above! Well, it was too late to do anything about it now.

God extended his goblet to a cherub and returned his eyes to his own world, which was infinite. He would leave his latest creations puzzling over their little universe, their minds imprisoned by time and space, their limited thoughts requiring everything to have a beginning and an end. In what they called a billion years he might retune the power of their multiplying urge. He was fond of the clever little dicks, who could see many things except their own insignificance.

TWO

Virgin Territory

....

I will dine nowhere without your consent although with my
present feelings I might be trusted with fifty virgins naked
in a dark room.

Lord Nelson writing from Spithead to Emma Hamilton on
Sunday, 22 February 1801

....

Virginibus Pueresque

During World War Two, *The Bedside Esquire* published
'An Idea for a Story' by André Maurois. He was a Parisian
who had escaped after the fall of France in 1940 to
America, the biographer indiscriminately of Shelley and
Professor Alexander Fleming, the author in the earlier
war of an amiable British send-up, *Les Silences du
colonel Bramble*. His literary idea was substituting the
satisfaction of hunger and thirst for the satisfaction of
sexual desire.

André Maurois, like God, was puzzled that the simple
physical need for sex should have aroused such complex
emotions. Furthermore, why should sex have occasioned
a predominance of artistic masterpieces since civilisation
began seriously in the twelfth century? He answered
himself that love expressed the harmony of two human
beings, while the satisfaction of hunger and thirst was
egotistic. If slaking your thirst or filling your belly were

7

pleasant, or even possible, only when achieved between two people, then hunger and thirst would have inspired overpowering passions and filled the Louvre.

André Maurois developed his idea by imagining an island with its population equipped on the right arm with a breast and nipple. This was always decently covered, to be exposed only when couples were alone to suck each other's delicious and life-sustaining liquid; meanwhile, they invited their friends round to copulate as we invite people to dinner. (Admittedly, some people now invite friends round for both, but all authors are children of their times.) Suckers who grew tired of one flavour brought anguish to their suppliers by discovering a tastier source, though some couples thirsted for each other faithfully for years. Descriptions of copulation enlivened their children's books, but descriptions of mutual feeding were outrageously condemned as obscene.

In the end, André Maurois decided not to write the story at all.

The transference of our most compelling passion from the urogenital to the alimentary tract, as André Maurois envisaged it, would not much incommode mankind. The world would be inspired by God's afterthought of equating an orgasm with digesting a nice steak and chips, and vice versa. Nobody would eat in public at all, but you could watch them do it on shady videos. Children would enjoy sexy television until bedtime, when the adults would settle down to mouth-watering cookery programmes. Aspiring women would freely copulate with their bosses, but lunch with them only secretly. A man would casually ask a girl to bed, but an invitation to dinner would incur calculation and persuasion. A wedding breakfast would be strictly private, but everyone would join in the honeymoon.

The Church would certainly declare a box of choc-

8

olates a heinous temptation, and ordain that eating a boiled egg not spooned from the saucepan of your usual cook was sinful. The Church – God's public relations subsidiary – was muddled from the start over the divine inspiration of creating humanity's most powerful passion to ensure a flow of more men and women. The Church narrow-mindedly declared this passion immoral, unless applied specifically for this purpose. Chastity became part of the job for priests, monks and nuns. The Puritans even castigated sex during pregnancy, because sex was exclusively for reproduction and as a pointless bit of fun invited damnation.

Such sweeping condemnation unkindly obliged conscientious mortals to perform the first night upon the marital stage without any rehearsals. Until the end of the seventeenth century, this drama was anyway semi-public. The wedding guests conducted the couple to their four-poster with many a jolly, appropriate joke, drawing the bed-curtains and leaving, to restart the show the next morning over breakfast. The bride always went to bed wearing gloves. When she lost her virginity, the gloves were off.

In the Middle Ages, as in the Victorian Age, prudery rubbed the naked shoulder of carnality. Songs celebrating marriage were robustly obscene, and marriage feasts provoked all-round sexual frolicking. Strip shows were unblushingly staged at receptions for kings and princes, with the excuse that they were *tableaux vivants* reproducing the Judgment of Paris. 'And there were also three very handsome girls, representing quite naked syrens, and one saw their beautiful turgid, separate, round, and hard breasts, which was a very pleasant sight, and they recited little motets and bergerettes; and near them several deep-toned instruments were playing fine melodies,' wrote the reporter of Louis XI's arrival at Paris in 1461.

9

The Church was so enthusiastic about virginity that it built handsome nunneries in high-walled grounds securely to accommodate it. Until the Reformation, these refuges shielded many daughters of noble and landed families.

Marriage is a deceptive landmark in the virgin territory created by God for reproduction. An unforeseen complication was its being founded not upon sex, but money. Under the untouchable principle of primogeniture, the eldest son inherited all, to propagate the line; getting rid of daughters invoked hefty dowries, money which preferably could be used to provide further families for penniless younger sons.

Many girls settled submissively to a shaven head and a life of prayer and porridge as an alternative to marrying under orders men they did not know and might not like at all. The bossy ones, who became abbesses, could delight in vigorously wielding a power far more sweeping than that of your everyday ladyship. When the nunneries were abolished by Henry VIII by 1535, the financial rebound on well-daughtered families was painful. For the next two centuries, younger sons had either to trap an heiress or join the army or build the Empire; a fifth of them were condemned to die old bachelors. The daughters, if themselves insufficiently priced and desperate for a husband with money, were overwhelmed with the importance of their own virginity; they needed painstakingly to preserve it, because everyone jibs at spending on shop-soiled goods.

The notion of romantic love inspiring marriage was in such times gravely suspect and ridiculous. How could any couple in such a state of mental derangement make an unregrettable choice of a lifetime companion? Wiser eyes among kinsmen and counsellors could coolly select a reliable housekeeper and mother. How fortunate were Romeo and Juliet, to be spared by suicide a union forged in such excitement and violence, flamed by a passion which would have later mystified both of them, as a nice young couple in Verona. Think of them doing the equivalent of the washing-up, and would Romeo have changed the baby's nappies?

In 1776, Samuel Johnson was arguing that 'marriages would in general be as happy, and often more so, if they were all made by the Lord Chancellor' – sitting on the Woolsack and weighing up the bride and bridegroom like the evidence, with no appeal against his judgment. But early that century, the Church had begun to admit that holy matrimony was also a contract, which the wife must submissively obey but which required the husband equally to extend love and fidelity; and though children should honour their father and their mother, a little reciprocality would be welcome.

By the century's end, romantic love had beaten a respectable path to the aisle, to the benefit of the romantic novelists – mainly female – who filled the spreading shelves of the circulating libraries. Newly built assembly rooms at Bath and similar sanitary places brought the pleasant discovery to young people that sex flowed in spa water, while in the developing London season mating became as deadly purposeful as shooting in the others.

For the propertyless classes, a church wedding in Dr Johnson's time was an expensive luxury. Couples joined and separated as they wished, like today. If they cared to split ceremoniously, the man took the woman to market with her neck in a halter and auctioned her among the mares and cows, raising a few guineas or perhaps only a few pence (consolingly, it was generally a put-up job, with the buyer in the act).

Lone mothers with bastards were cared for by the workhouse. The (unreliable) annual illegitimacy rate under Elizabeth I was 4 per cent, falling under the Puritans to half a per cent, and rising to 6 per cent under

George III. Nowadays, 33 per cent of British babies are bastards, 44 per cent of our pregnant women are unmarried and over 100,000 of them every year are in their teens.

Even in the 1660s, magistrates busied themselves shifting the maintenance of the child from the parish to the father, if traceable. Today's pursued fathers can console themselves that early in the seventeenth century both of the unmarried parents were whipped in public, then were sat half-naked in the stocks under a sign denouncing their fornication. The workhouse has been replaced by the welfare state, which causes sporadic outrage among taxpayers, who are sensitive about paying for a sin which they have not committed. But nobody now bothers much about bastards, which is admirably civilised: the surest way to make people less sinful is to reduce the number of sins.

The Church had got its hands on marriage in the thirteenth century, but it was not until the canons of 1606 that the Church created it indissoluble, made adultery and fornication punishable, disinherited bastards, and obliged the marital state to start only between eight in the morning and noon, in churches and not inns. All was tidied up in 1753 by Lord Hardwicke's Marriage Act, which obliged the bride and groom to sign the parish register and ordained as illegal marriages under twenty-one without parental consent (there was always Gretna Green, first stop in exempt Scotland). There were puzzles: this illegal under-age marriage was still indissoluble; and remarriage was permissible after a spouse's seven-year absence (presumed dead), though on the wanderer's return the first wife could reclaim her abandoned marital property, if preferred.

Milton saw through the quickly fading and often tattered veils of sexual delight that marriage was firstly for 'the apt and cheerful conversation of man with woman, to comfort and refresh him against the solitary life'. Can it? Over the past twenty years in Britain, marriages have declined by 16 per cent but divorces more than doubled. We now celebrate joyfully 375,410 marriages a year and, probably equally so, 168,249 divorces, plus an incalculable number of unwed ruptures. This suggests that men and women, essential sexually to each other, are unsuited to live together. The point was made forcefully by James Thurber and E. B. White in *Is Sex Necessary?* of 1929:

> A woman ... knows most of it by intuition and the
> rest she has learned from her mother. But to
> suppose that a husband should know, offhand,
> whether a chest of drawers with woollens or
> dimity in it goes to the attic or the basement is
> ridiculous. You might as well expect him to
> understand, without long, careful instruction, why
> one tea towel is used for the china and another for
> the glassware.

Virgin birth is an odd conception. The biblical one was a fiction of the fussy Church, which could not allow Jesus to be born by an activity so rude as copulation. His was not the only one – Attis, a god of vegetation in Asia Minor, was conceived by Nana, the daughter of a river god, by putting a pomegranate down her bosom. Attis later castrated himself and was turned into a pine tree.

Parthenogenesis – virgin birth in Greek – is a privilege bestowed by God only upon aphids and honeybees. In summer, the wingless female greenfly produces without any outside help generations of wingless female green-flies, a quick and efficient way of increasing the world's aphids without necessitating the presence of males, who are busy sucking sap elsewhere. In the hive, the bee family buzzes with queen, workers and the drones. The fat baritone drones are all male, all fertile, and have all been given birth by the queen in virginal self-sufficiency.

Generations of biologists had been poking, freezing, boiling and convulsing the unfertilised eggs of such inviting species as the sea urchin, which conceives disinterestedly with its eggs floating about in the sea, and of bracken, which would not sprout at all did its eggs not secrete malic acid to attract the wafting sperm of other bracken. These scientists were seeking to produce their own virgin birth, but enjoyed no more success than a few fatherless frogs hopping around their laboratories.

Virgin birth is now famously available to all virgins, of whatever age and sexual inclination, making further nonsense of God's bestowal of the overpoweringly delightful sexual urge.

With artificial insemination, predominantly applied to long-deflowered virgins, the parents enjoy nothing. The only passion aroused in their child's conception is experienced by the donor achieving ejaculation, comparable to that similarly aroused in a prize bull. The incidental emotions, pondered by André Maurois, occasioned in a woman by *in vitro* fertilisation are no more complex than those of having her ears syringed. And what artistic masterpieces has the technique's repeated successes inspired for the world's galleries? Botticelli's *Birth of Venus* will have to do for the lot.

Contrariwise, contraception, which has lightened human sexual problems since Colonel Condom first marched into the eighteenth century, liberally permits the complex passions and artistic inspiration of sexual arousal while despising the reason for which this stimulus was created. Mankind's biological multiplication table has become reduced to nought times nought making nought. God will have much to exercise his mind when, in a billion of our years, he turns his attention back to our cosy universe from whatever else he is thinking about.

The Age of Chivalry

Chivalry is basically the rescue of virgins by knights errant from dragons. This was exemplified by England's patron saint, George, and publicised by Sir Edward Burne-Jones, whose painting of the event now hangs at Sydney, in the land of natural chivalry where no Sheila goes long without warm banter and cool refreshment.

Though St George and the dragon are as English as steak and kidney, their story is widespread from Japan to Senegal and Scandinavia: a hydra-headed monster periodically threatens to gobble up the local population, unless some tasty virgin is served him. The victim's turn falls to the king's daughter, but some humble young man slays the beast and wins the princess. In the Maldive Islands, when the evil jinn appeared as a ship of burning lamps, the virgin was left overnight in a seaside temple, to be found in the morning deflowered and dead, until someone saved her comparatively effortlessly by reciting the Koran.

Chivalry is the romantic aurora brightening the sky of the Dark Ages. Its admirable sentiments of compassion, sacrifice, honour and fidelity were emitted by the nobility, and not available to the lower classes, who had no civic duties beyond touching their forelocks. The equality of man was certainly accepted in the Middle Ages, but only unobtrusively after death.

Religion in Europe of the thirteenth century dominated all thought and all feelings. Which was reasonable, when there was only the Good Lord to deliver us from plague, pestilence and famine, from battle and murder, and from sudden death. Life was short, humanity could feel the warmth of the flames of Hell and scent the freshness of the Heavenly pastures, and needed to pick its way on earth adroitly between the two prospects. Next in mental dominance of the medieval world was chivalry. The ascending orders of knighthood were the floors in the structure of feudal society, which had been built indestructibly by God.

The sentiments of chivalry were equally religious and lecherous:

> It is sensuality transformed into the craving for self-sacrifice, into the desire of the male to show his courage, to incur danger, to be strong, to suffer and to bleed before his lady-love . . . The man will not be content merely to suffer, he will want to save from danger, or from suffering, the object of his desire. A more vehement stimulus is added to the primary motif: its chief feature will be that of defending imperilled virginity – in other words, that of ousting the rival. This, then, is the essential theme of chivalrous love poetry; the young hero, delivering the virgin. The sexual motif is always behind it . . .

perceived Johan Huizinga's *Waning of the Middle Ages*.

Jousting was sexy. The knights wore the veils and dresses of their adoring supporters, who were incited to perform a strip-tease at the lists, hurling their finery excitedly to the combatants. The thirteenth-century troubadours sang of a nobleman's wife who sent three of her shirts to three knights, to don instead of their armour at the morrow's tournament. Two wisely declined, but the third slept in the shirt, passionately kissed it, got badly wounded in it, and won the sexual favours of the lady, who wore it torn and blood-stained over her gown at the jousting feast. All this puzzled her husband.

16

In 1348 the Black Death unchivalrously spoiled the fun by killing off half the inhabitants of Europe.

Wise and Foolish Virgins

St Matthew 25: 1–12:

> Then shall the kingdom of heaven be likened unto ten virgins, which took their lamps, and went forth to meet the bridegroom. And five of them were wise, and five were foolish. They that were foolish took their lamps, and took no oil with them: But the wise took oil in their vessels with their lamps. While the bridegroom tarried, they all slumbered and slept. And at midnight there was a cry made, Behold, the bridegroom cometh; go ye out to meet him. Then all those virgins arose, and trimmed their lamps. And the foolish said unto the wise, Give us of your oil; for our lamps are gone out. But the wise answered, saying, Not so; lest there be not enough for us and you: but go ye rather to them that sell, and buy for yourselves. And while they went to buy, the bridegroom came; and they that were ready went in with him to the marriage: and the door was shut. Afterward came also the other virgins, saying, Lord, Lord, open to us. But he answered and said, Verily I say unto you, I know you not.

This is not the shiniest illustration of Jesus's brilliant moralistic copywriting. Why did the wise virgins not display a decent Christian spirit, trim their wicks and share their oil with the unwise ones? Were the unwise only ignorant virgins? The wise clearly knew the bridegroom's ways, that he was the sort of man who would be late for his own wedding, or they would never have cluttered themselves up with cruses of oil. To send unwise virgins safely venturing out after midnight, and at that hour successfully buying some more oil, indicates that life in the Holy Land was more convenient than in England's green and pleasant one.

The wise Catherine of Siena of the mid-fourteenth century, the steadfast virgin saint, was the youngest of twenty children of a cloth-dyer. She persistently refused marriage, and instead nursed the sick in hospital, like Britain's unhaloed saintly virgin, Florence Nightingale. St Catherine was flattered with manipulating the home-coming of Gregory XI from Avignon to Rome, and thus the papacy's escape from characteristic French meddling. When Pope Gregory died in 1378, she nagged impartially his successor Urban VI not to be so beastly to everyone, and the rulers of Europe to accept Urban as Pope instead of the rival French bishop installed at Avignon. St Catherine died in 1380, but her letters and dialogues continued to inspire the world until their last publication in 1947: she dictated everything, not having learned to write. Her head is still in Siena, but her body is 231 kilometres away in the church of Santa Maria sopra Minerva in Rome.

St Colette was a more tiresomely enthusiastic virgin. Copulation revolted her. She shuddered with repugnance at saints who had been married. She refused any but virgins to join her congregation, though the screening must have been difficult. She lived in horror of flies, slugs and ants, of dirt and stinks, of the heat and glow from the fire, enduring only candlelight. (She was a severe obsessional neurotic, poor dear.) The Church applauded her. It did not care if the worthy reverence it afforded virginity ballooned into the fanatical. The Church preferred that any exuberant religious emotion should bounce and burst harmlessly in such ecstatic fancies, rather than threaten to explode its doctrinal foundations.

It was once unwise to be a young virgin in Cairo between the sixth and sixteenth of August, because one of them was beautifully adorned and then cast into the rising Nile, to ensure plentiful watering of the crops. Nor was it wise in the Middle Ages for any young woman to accept an invitation to sleep the night with a saintly man, to test his virtue. There was a fashion for holy men to prove their holiness by mixing ashes with their food, or like the hermit St Giles, shot by an arrow misfired at a hind, to pray God that his wound would heal slowly and so exhibit his patience. After a night on the test-bed, the man enduring this unobserved sexual temptation would in the morning proclaim his unscathed virginity to the world, but I fancy most relevantly to the Marines.

There's the vulva, the vagina and the jolly perineum,
And the hymen in the case of lots of brides,

wrote A. P. Herbert, in his poem starting: 'The portion of a woman that appeals to man's depravity', composed on the flyleaf of a ship's doctor's gynaecology textbook during a boring voyage.

Why such fuss about this minor anatomical structure? 'Every harlot was a virgin once,' summarised Blake.

The Virgin Islands

About 100 islands in the West Indies, between 17° to 18° 50' N and 64° 10' to 65° 30' W, running east from Puerto Rico to the Sombrero Passage between the Atlantic and the Caribbean. They lie in the trade-wind belt and have a subtropical climate. Britain rules forty-six (eleven inhabited), comprising 29 square miles with a population of 16,108, their industries rum, stone-crushing, tourists and off-shore funds, the Governor appointed by the

Crown. The USA has the rest (three inhabited), making 132 square miles with a population of 101,809, the Governor democratically elected. The USA bought them from Denmark in 1917 for $25m, because of their strategic importance *en route* to the Panama Canal. They return a delegate to Congress, but he is not allowed to vote. The Virgin Islands were discovered by Columbus in 1493 and christened in honour of seafaring St Ursula and her 11,000 virginal companions.

The Virginals

The earliest harpsichord. A portable oblong box with the strings, plucked by crow-quills, running parallel to the keyboard. It was a favourite domestic instrument of the sixteenth and early seventeenth centuries, until superseded by the harp-shaped spinet. The name perhaps arises from its handiness as a means of musical expression by young ladies: the first printed virginals music in 1611 was *Parthenia*, 'Maidens' Songs', pavans and galliards by William Byrd, John Bull and Orlando Gibbons. In 1547, Henry VIII left a 'a Virginal that goeth with a whele without playing upon', his prototype of the 1897 Pianola.

THREE

Our Royal Virgin

. . . .

And to me it shall be a full satisfaction both for the memorial
of my name, and for my glory also, if when I shall let my
last breath, it be ingraven upon my Marble Tombe, Here
lyeth ELIZABETH, which raigned a Virgin, and dyed a
Virgin.

Elizabeth I, speech to Parliament, 1559

. . . .

A Broken Home

Queen Elizabeth I had a difficult childhood.

Before her birth, her uncle Arthur had married a Spanish girl at the age of fourteen, gone to live in Wales and
swiftly died from flu. His brother Henry – a strapping
eleven-year-old with splendid prospects – instantly got
engaged to his widow Catherine, who otherwise would
have gone home to her parents in Aragon. They did not
marry for seven years, until 1509 (there was some weari-
some niggling over the dowry). She was then twenty-
three and he was eighteen and had just become the King
of England.

A marriage which a man contracts before puberty is
unlikely to last until senility, but the happy couple
nearly attained their silver wedding before divorcing in
May 1533. Catherine had five children, but in those
times of perilous childbirth, even for the most pampered

patients, only one survived – so disappointingly for father, a girl, Mary.

Henry had earlier taken a fancy to the Duke of Norfolk's niece, vivacious Anne, aged fifteen and just home from the French court, where her father was the ambassador. She was the mistress of the poet Sir Thomas Wyatt, who wrote:

> And wilt thou leave me thus,
> That hath given thee my heart
> Never for to depart . . .

despite which, in 1527 and aged twenty, she bettered herself by exchanging him for the King.

Henry showered wealth on her lucky old father, Sir Thomas Boleyn, and made him the Earl of Wiltshire. The pair married four months before Henry's divorce from Catherine came through – impatiently and secretly, because Anne was already pregnant with Elizabeth, born in Greenwich on 7 September 1533. Two years and four months later Elizabeth had a brother, but stillborn.

Henry's second marriage was less successful than his first. Within six months the bridegroom's ardour had lost its tumescence, mocking the magnificent celebration of the bride in Westminster Hall on the newly-weds' first Whit Sunday. Catherine had meanwhile gone to live in the country, took to religion, and died aged fifty from an aortic aneurysm (perhaps acquired by infection with her husband's syphilis) on 7 January 1536.

Family matters then started to shift fast.

On 1 May 1536, Henry abandoned Anne abruptly at a tournament in Greenwich. He had spied her dropping her hanky to some man in the lists. He had already set the private eyes on her, who reported that she had committed incest with her brother George and had enjoyed sex with four commoners – three times with

Mark Smeaton, musician and deft dancer, whom she hid in her cupboard of dried fruits.

Her husband was furious. The day after the tournament, the lot were locked up in the Tower. On 12 May, the four lovers were convicted of high treason, and on 15 May so were Anne and George. Henry was showing that he was a man who would stand no nonsense. The Duke of Norfolk did the dirty on his niece by presiding over the judges, and her ennobled and enriched father inclined to the husband's view. The court later tore up all the evidence. On 19 May Anne was beheaded on Tower Green and on 30 May the widower married Jane Seymour.

The next year, the new bride died unneedful of the headsman, but in October she had given Henry a much desired son, Edward. The refreshed widower married another Anne, of a reliable German Protestant family in Cleves. He never much liked her looks, and being a practical man made plain before the wedding that the divorce would follow, which he accomplished speedily without bothering to copulate with her.

In August 1540, Henry married another niece of the Duke of Norfolk, the jolly, fat, nineteen-year-old Catherine Howard. She had already been fornicated regularly by her music master Henry Mannock, and had become accepted among their friends as the wife of Francis Dereham, a rich retainer of her grandmother the dowager Duchess, who presided at Horsham in Norfolk. When Francis Dereham was away in Ireland, Catherine decided to marry properly her cousin Thomas Culpepper of Kent, but she met Henry at the Bishop's Palace and her friends all pressed her to marry *him*, sensing something in it for themselves.

King and noblewoman wed secretly in July 1540. The next year, with the help of her cousin Lady Rochford, Catherine equally secretly met Thomas Culpepper in

Pontefract, while openly appointing Francis Dereham her secretary. The silly girl should have known better. Her maid sneaked on her Pontefract trip to her husband, who instantly set the private eyes on her. They enlightened the King about her prenuptial larks, but could produce no hard evidence of the post- ones. No matter, said Henry impatiently, beheading Culpepper and Dereham on the spot, then Lady Rochford (who had gone mad) and his unsatisfactory wife on 13 February 1542.

On 12 July 1543, Henry married thirty-one-year-old, already twice-widowed, placid, rich Catherine Parr. The King was fifty-two, with varicose ulcers, bone sinuses, possibly tertiary syphilis, immensely fat and needing a block and tackle to get upstairs. Catherine wanted to marry instead Thomas, the brother of Jane Seymour, but diplomatically let herself be embraced by the royal arms. She was obliged to wait for her desired husband until three months after Henry's death in January 1548, probably then emitting the deepest sigh of relief in matrimonial history.

Princess Elizabeth had matured amid this marital mayhem nursing her own wound. When she was two, Henry had declared Elizabeth and her half-sister Mary illegitimate. There were lingering effects of Catherine of Aragon's divorce, which had occasioned her father considerable extraneous difficulties, like changing the country's religion. And Anne's conduct clearly necessitated her marriage being declared invalid as well as having her head chopped off. Demoted to Lady Elizabeth, she grew up ingloriously in Hertfordshire, steadfastly pursuing Latin and Greek taught by Roger Ascham, Cambridge don and adept archer.

After fifteen-year-old King Edward VI's death from tuberculosis in 1553 occurred the deadly fiasco of Lady Jane Grey. She was Henry VIII's widowed sister Mary's granddaughter – tight entanglements make the Tudor tapestry dreadfully difficult in its unpicking. Lady Jane was severely brought up, well educated, a fluent linguist, a staunch Protestant, who was aged fifteen and just married, against her will, to the Duke of Northumberland's fourth son, Lord Guildford Dudley. The idea behind the match was to change the succession from the Tudors to the Dudleys, but the only result was getting the happy couple beheaded in 1554.

After Lady Jane's reign of a fortnight, Elizabeth rode alongside Mary when she triumphantly entered the City of London as Queen. Mary was the English face of Catholicism, which stared in horror at heretics; Elizabeth of Protestantism, which gazed appalled at candlelit Masses; and each when in power liberally burnt their opponents to save their souls. The glories of religions do not shine brilliantly with a readiness to see each other's point of view. How less painful are opposing politicians than rancorously antagonistic priests, because politicians shrewdly spot their rivals' good ideas and pinch them for their own.

This Catholic–Protestant schism expectedly dominated the marriage prospects of the two princesses. Their choice was limited and involuntary. Royal offspring given in matrimony was the international extension of businesslike family alliances. The Crowned Heads' Marriage Agency flourished until Queen Victoria, who graciously freed her daughter Louise to wed the son of a coroneted duke. Louise was the first princess to marry outside a reigning house since Henry VIII's sister Mary (see above), the widow of Louis XII of France, who married in Paris in 1514 the square-jawed Duke of Suffolk, who already had a wife, but this was conveniently overcome by a papal bull and by Henry being 'pacified by large gifts of money'.

Mary I ascended aged thirty-seven. A year later, she married at Winchester King Philip II of Spain, who was plump, fair, with full lips, a goatee beard and a soft moustache, aged twenty-seven and the human Gibraltar of Catholicism. He had landed three days previously at Southampton, when the couple first met. The marriage did not detain him long in England. A busy man among the other countries of Europe, he returned to Spain the following summer, went back to the wife in the spring of 1557, got her to declare war against the French – who swiftly took Calais after two centuries' English occupation – and left again in July. He had found fourteen months in his wife's cold country long enough.

Before Philip's first departure, Mary announced that she was pregnant, thus joyfully securing the Catholic succession. Ambassadorial announcements were prepared in diplomatic French (with enough space after the hopeful *fil* for a regrettable *-le*). The country became excited on 30 April 1555 with bells and bonfires proclaiming the birth. But it was a pseudocyesis. The phantom pregnancy was implanted in her mind by lack of menstruation and abdominal swelling from the fluid occasioned by her illness. Mary died in 1558 from ovarian carcinoma, with Calais lying in her heart.

Elizabeth had earlier joined the royal sexual progress at the age of fourteen. Though Mary was insisting that Mark Smeaton from the fruit-cupboard was Elizabeth's father, surely everyone could see the resemblance?

Assailants of the Queen's Virginity

1 1548. *Thomas Seymour.* Later, *Baron Seymour of Sudley.*
 Age: 40. Elizabeth's age: 14.
 Appearance: handsome, red-headed and red-bearded.
 Attraction: sexy, fascinating, reckless, amusing.

Thomas Seymour was the brother of Jane Seymour who secretly married the queen-dowager, Catherine Parr (see more above). After a splendid diplomatic, military and naval career (this was long before talent could be replaced by specialisation), he became Lord High Admiral, a position which he bettered by going fifty-fifty in the spoils of the busy Bristol Channel pirates. He owned much of Wiltshire.

His brother Edward, the Duke of Somerset, was Protector for the nine-year-old Edward VI; the ambitious Thomas schemed in an unfraternal manner to turn King against Protector, as he wished the youthful monarch to marry Lady Jane Grey, aged ten (see even more above).

'He amused himself with the Princess,' Lytton Strachey describes Seymour's relationship with young Elizabeth. 'Bounding into her room in the early morning, he would fall upon her, while she was in her bed or just out of it, with peals of laughter, would seize her in his arms and tickle her, and slap her buttocks, and crack a ribald joke. These proceedings continued for several weeks, when Catherine Parr, getting wind of them, sent Elizabeth to live elsewhere.'

When Catherine Parr made Seymour a widower in 1548, he pressingly offered marriage to the stepdaughter whom he had submitted to princess abuse. The match would strengthen him against his brother in seeking power at the top. Elizabeth turned him down. He persisted. Rumours flew that she was pregnant, which she wrote bitterly to the Protector to deny. Further embarrassment was spared her in March 1549, when for all his trouble the Lord High Admiral was conveniently beheaded for treason. The King fired the Protector in 1550, and beheaded him too on Tower Hill in 1552. They were times when heads rolled like an upset apple-cart.

2 1553. *Edward Courtenay*. Later, *Earl of Devonshire*.
Age: 27. Elizabeth's age: 20.
Appearance: pale, fair-haired and gormless.
Attraction: modesty, scholarship (he translated an Italian devotional treatise in 1548, but it had to wait until 1856 for publication).

In 1554, Sir Thomas Wyatt (the son of Anne Boleyn's poet) led a revolt against Queen Mary I. It was ignited by the Queen's impending marriage to Philip of Spain, it flamed in Kent and was extinguished at Temple Bar. Sir Thomas's head went on 11 April, followed by his drawing and quartering and his decoration of several street corners in London.

Sir Thomas had plotted for Elizabeth to marry Catholic Edward Courtenay, who was the son of the Marquis of Exeter (beheaded in 1538), and vaguely related to Henry VIII. Had his revolt blown Queen Mary from the throne, Edward would have been Protestant Elizabeth's inoffensive Catholic consort. Edward had previously been encouraged to marry Queen Mary herself, but when he lost his suit to the King of Spain he allowed himself to be reorientated. Elizabeth took to him, but he was not passionate about the affair, and anyway he 'lived dissolutely' – which was reasonable, as he had been locked up in the Tower from the age of twelve. Such marital intentions merited his own beheading, but he escaped with exile, to die the next year in Padua.

3 1560. *Robert Dudley*. Later, *Earl of Leicester*.
Age: 28. Elizabeth's age: 27.
Appearance: tall, handsome, swarthy ('the gypsy'), beak-nosed, dark-eyed, delicate skin, neat beard and handlebar moustache, lovely legs.
Attraction: crack horseman, ballroom star, a fan of the theatre, read books, exuded sparkling

chat, spoke Italian and was deeply concerned about modern architecture.

On Sunday 8 September 1560, Lady Amye Dudley, who had been married to Robert for ten years, was found by the servants dead with a broken neck at the bottom of the staircase at Comnor Hall, just west of Oxford. The inquest verdict was accidental death, but tongues wagged like the pennants of the Queen's knights. Everyone knew that Amye's husband had driven her to suicide; or had poisoned her, with the connivance of Queen Elizabeth, with whom he was having a vigorous affair. Perhaps everyone was right: there were pointers to a plot in the Spanish national archives at Simancas in Valladolid.

Dudley's grandfather had been beheaded by Henry VIII and his father by Mary I. He was 'a light and greedy man' whom nobody liked nor trusted. The new Queen fancied him royally. She made him Master of the Horse, Knight of the Garter, High Steward of Cambridge University and tickled him in public. He was spied kissing her in her coach, and in her bedroom one morning handing over her shift. The buzz was that they were going to marry, and equally loudly that she was pregnant. William Cecil, Elizabeth's Secretary of State, was against the marriage because he was already seeing his influence upon her eroded by the suitor's. Dudley resourcefully sought Spanish support for the match: his offer was Elizabeth's abject ackowledgement of papal supremacy, but King Philip wanted it in writing first.

Presumptuous Dudley sometimes displeased the Queen, and they squabbled. Perhaps she was anyway just pretending. In 1563 she suggested to him an alternative – becoming husband to Mary, Queen of Scots, for whom a dozen kings, archdukes and dukes were queuing up at Holyrood. Mary chose instead Lord Darnley, who was weak, poor, arrogant and debauched. These defects

29

swiftly caused a marital breech, which occasioned her chief minister, the Italian David Rizzio, being dragged from her presence on 9 March 1566 and stabbed to death in the next room. She blew her husband up in Edinburgh the following February, with the help of the Earl of Bothwell, whom she married three months later. Dudley was well out of it.

When he turned forty in 1573, Dudley secretly married Lady Sheffield, whose husband he was suspected of poisoning. Five years later he married, if bigamously, Lettice, widow of the Earl of Essex, himself widely believed to have completed Dudley's hat-trick of poisoned spouses. Elizabeth was only temporarily put out at such naughtiness. In 1588 she gave Dudley command as Captain-General of the forces assembled at Tilbury to face the Spanish invasion; on 4 September he died suddenly in Oxford, reportedly, in the family tradition, from poison intended for his wife.

> 4 1564. *Sir Christopher Hatton.*
> Age: 24. Elizabeth's age: 31.
> Appearance: stout, florid, thick brown hair, neat
> beard, handlebar moustache.
> Attraction: impressive in the saddle and on the
> dance-floor, a charmer, an amusing talker.

A Northampton lad who became its MP and the Queen's parliamentary mouthpiece. Education: Oxford, no degree but made Chancellor of the University by the Queen in 1588; Inner Temple, not called to the Bar but made Lord Chancellor by the Queen in 1587.

He became a gentleman-pensioner and Captain of the Bodyguard. In 1578, the Queen commanded the Bishop of Ely (whom she loathed) to surrender to Sir Christopher his estate at Ely Place, Holborn, for the yearly rent of £10, ten carts of hay and a midsummer rose. His name now sparkles at Hatton Garden, alley of the diamond trade.

He was an adoring confidant and passionate correspondent, sending her a talisman with specific instructions to hang it between the royal dugs. Everyone whispered that he was having it off with the Queen, and in 1584 Mary Queen of Scots charged him outright with it; this gave relish to his finalising her execution three years later. He died in debt aged 51, a bachelor, and lay in St Paul's.

> 5 1570. *Edward de Vere.* Later (aged twelve) *Earl of Oxford.*
> Age: 20. Elizabeth's age: 37.
> Appearance: 'Italianate'.
> Attraction: another virtuoso of the saddle and the dancing-pumps.

Oxford was spendthrift, quarrelsome, arrogant, affected in speech and gesture and inclined to violence, but the Queen loved him and gave him paying jobs at court.

He wrote poetry.

> If women could be fair and yet not fond,
> Or that their love were firm, not fickle still,
> I would not marvel that they make men bond
> By service long to purchase their good will . . .

Which the coquettish Queen may have found a little near the bone.

In 1571 he married Ann, the eldest daughter of William Cecil, his guardian, in whose home he had killed the cook. Oxford surlily disowned her first pregnancy, remained uncaring of his wife and three daughters, and after she died in childbed married a maid of honour with a rich father. In 1579 he had a terrible row with Sir Philip Sidney – soldier, poet, a fainter royal favourite, handsome with delicate mouth and eyebrows – who called him a puppy. Such violent tantrums finally threw him into disgrace at court, but he did his bit against the Armada.

6 1581: *Sir Walter Raleigh.*
Age: 29. Elizabeth's age: 48.
Appearance: ruddy, dark-haired, goatee beard, splendid bearing.
Attraction: dashing.

A son of Glorious Devon (Sidmouth), his boyhood is well known. He arrived at court as a protégé of Dudley, the Earl of Leicester, bearing dispatches from Ireland, where Raleigh had just killed off six hundred Spanish and Italian prisoners in County Kerry. The Queen took an instant fondness to him, to the fury of Sir Christopher Hatton.

Raleigh was sure of himself, full of himself, quick-tempered and showy; everyone hated him, but toadied up to appease the royal affection. Elizabeth made him Captain of the Guard and Lord Warden of the Stannaries and bestowed upon him lucrative monopolies – wines, woollen broadcloth, playing cards. She awarded him broad acres in England and broader in Ireland, and gave him a house in the Strand by throwing out the resident bishop (this time of Durham). She was so generous towards him that she scandalised even her hardened courtiers.

In 1584, Raleigh was vouchsafed a patent for mounting an expedition to acquire unknown lands in America in the Queen's name. It sweepingly took the seaboard from Florida to Newfoundland, which the Queen felt appropriate to name Virginia. Raleigh wisely never went there himself, for the place was discovered uninhabitable. Several expeditions to colonise it were abandoned, though it provided Europe with its amiable potato and sinister tobacco. Raleigh's other mistake was making maid of honour Bessy Throckmorton pregnant in 1592, for which the Queen furiously threw both into the Tower. She repented, they were released, he married her, but was banned the court and went to live quietly in Dorset.

Three years later, Raleigh led an expedition searching for gold up the River Orinoco (now in Venezuela). He found no gold, but brought home tales of a mysterious native arrow poison, which paralysed but did not kill, a syrup from the creeper *curare*. This third innovation now provides safe surgical flaccidity under light anaesthesia upon the operating-tables of the world.

James I became King, his mind already set against Raleigh by Cecil. Raleigh's trial at Winchester for conspiracy restored his popularity in the country but condemned him to death. In December 1603 he was reprieved upon the scaffold; he relieved domestic imprisonment in the Bloody Tower with his wife and son by performing chemical experiments and writing the history of the world. In 1616, he was released for another expedition to the Orinoco, but the Spanish objected to his burning down their new settlement of San Tomás, and he was beheaded on the old Winchester sentence in Old Palace Yard, Westminster, on 29 October 1618. In the Elizabethan court tradition, he was a poet:

> . . . the dark and silent grave,
> When we have wander'd all our ways,
> Shuts up the story of our days;
> But from this earth, this grave, this dust,
> My God shall raise me up, I trust.

7 1586. *Robert Devereux.* Later, *Earl of Essex.*
   Age: 20. Elizabeth's age: 53.
   Appearance: tall, handsome, pale, with a brown
   beard; ten years later, dissolute-looking with

bags under the eyes.
Attraction: boyish spirits, arrogant charm.

He was the Earl of Leicester's stepson. He was an instant favourite. He was made Master of the Horse (£1,500 a year), farmed the tax on sweet wines, and he played cards – or other games – alone with the Queen all night. 'My Lord cometh not to his own lodging till birds sing in the morning,' the neighbours noticed.

Essex was vain, extravagant, poor, touchy, impetuous, jealous. He quickly quarrelled with the pivotal favourite, Sir Walter Raleigh, and duelled in Marylebone Fields with a peripheral one, the handsome Charles Blount. Blount had worn tied to his sleeve the golden queen from Elizabeth's chessmen, with which she had rewarded his skill at tilting: 'Now I perceive that every fool must have a favour,' Essex commented sourly. Essex was slightly wounded in the combat. 'By God's death!' exclaimed Elizabeth at the news, 'it is fit that someone or other should take him down, and teach him better manners.' It was pleasant to see blood spilt over herself. And anyway, the two contestants soon became firm chums.

After Sir Philip Sidney's death at Zutphen in 1586, Essex married his widow (the daughter of Walsingham, the Queen's efficient counsellor and spymaster, who died without honours, only debts). This predictably infuriated the Queen, but she and Essex had so many rows and so many makings-up, he was so *naughty*! Essex returned to favour by 1593, won glory by beating the Spanish fleet and taking Cadiz in 1596, philandered among the ladies-in-waiting and made some of them pregnant, and in 1598 quarrelled with the Queen over appointing the new Lord Deputy of Ireland.

They were all standing up in the Council Chamber. He *turned his back on her*: unthinkable. She shouted: 'Go to the devil!' and deservedly boxed his ears. He *clap-*

34

ped his hand to his sword – phew! He shouted back: 'This is an outrage that I will not put up with! I would not have borne it from your father's hands.' They were separated by the Earl of Nottingham, who bundled him out of the room. But the pair were dancing again on Twelfth Night. Then she sent *him* to Ireland.

The English who had seized Irish land thought the natives absurd savages and oppressed them; the Irish, backed by Spanish soldiers and munitions, thought the English cruel and greedy and massacred them as opportunity presented. Essex did not improve the situation. After his defeat in Wicklow, he decimated his troops *pour encourager les autres*. He made a truce (renewable six weekly) with the rebellious Earl of Tyrone, he hurried home on 28 September 1599, early in the morning he galloped to the court – which was then on tour at Nonesuch in Essex – burst into the Queen's bedroom all muddy, kissed her hands passionately on his knees, and left her to carry on dressing.

The truce was not appreciated. Essex was stripped of his dignities, imprisoned, but freed after two months. On 8 February 1601 he had the wild idea of raising the citizens of London to oust the Queen's counsellors, on the 19th he was tried at Westminster Hall – prosecuted by Francis Bacon, an old friend for whom, when Bacon was a struggling barrister, he had strived to win the Queen's preferment – found guilty of high treason and on the 25th beheaded in the Tower. He wrote sonnets.

8 *Prospective Bridegrooms.*

> *Philip II of Spain.* Elizabeth turned down her
> sister's widower in 1559. Pope Paul IV anyway
> forbade the marriage: Elizabeth was illegitimate,
> and the crown was his to bestow, England being
> but a fief of the Holy See. Protestantism was
> henceforth in England synonymous with
> patriotism.

The *Archduke Charles*, Philip's nephew (he too pressed his suit in 1559; in 1564 he turned up again and was turned down again).

Don Carlos, son of Philip of Spain (aged eight).

Charles IX of France (when he was seventeen and Elizabeth was thirty-four).

'Mad' King Eric XIV of Sweden (who ended up with a peasant-girl).

The *Dukes of Aumale, Enghien, Holstein, Savoy* and *Saxony*.

The *Earls of Arran* and *Arundel*.

Sir William Pickering (a 'comely English gentleman').

Pope Sixtus V.

The *Duke of Anjou*, later *Henry III of France* (after Elizabeth asked for Calais back as a wedding-present, it was announced that the marriage would not now take place).

The *Duke of Alençon*, later Francis, *Duke of Anjou*, Henry III's youngest brother. The Duke was short, pock-marked, with a big nose. 'My frog,' said Elizabeth fondly. Their marriage was proposed in 1572, when he was eighteen and she was pushing forty. He had bright wits, amusing chat and ingratiating manners. In the summer of 1579 he paid a secret visit to England, which everyone knew about, at courtly functions having to hide behind tapestries. The Queen took to him hugely. He wrote her passionate letters and was back a couple of summers later, still in secret. She warned him their union would be barren, that having a child would kill her. He did not care. She gave him a big kiss after dinner at Whitehall Palace, she exchanged rings and to everyone's alarm announced they were getting married, but in the morning she had changed her mind. He was dreadfully upset, but she gave him her handkerchief to cry on. She wrote after he had sailed from Sandwich:

I grieve, yet dare not shew my discontent;
I love, and yet am forced to seem to hate;
I dote, but dare not what I ever meant;
I seem stark mute, yet inwardly doe prate;
I am, and am not – freeze, and yet I burn;
Since from myself my other self I turn.

Unfortunately for the suitor, a close alliance
with France was thought inexpedient after all.
When three summers later the frog died, she
plunged the court into mourning and felt
overwhelmingly sorry about it all.

The proposed marriage with a Catholic was not popular. The Puritans tiraded against it, and John Stubbe, a lawyer and MP for Yarmouth, respectfully enlightened the Queen in his pamphlet *The Discoverie of a gaping gulf whereinto England is like to be swallowed* about 'the sin and punishment thereof' – particularly when these were occasioned by a bride of her age. For which invasion of privacy he had his right hand chopped off. Stubbe immediately shouted 'God save the Queen!', respectfully removed his hat with his remaining hand and collapsed, before being re-placed in the Tower for an eighteen-month stretch. How our present haphazard royalty must regret losing these means of handling the paparazzi.

A Gynaecological Problem

'Fond, foolish, wanton, flibbergibs, tattlers, triflers, wavering, witless, without council, feeble, careless, rash, proud, dainty, tale-bearers, eavesdroppers, rumour-raisers, evil-tongued, worse-minded, and in every way doltified with the dregs of the devil's dunghill,' the Bishop of London gave his opinion of femininity in a

37

sermon before Queen Elizabeth (the Bishop 'became very unpopular owing to his arbitrary and unconciliatory disposition'). He prudently admitted from the pulpit that some women were wiser than many men, though he was supported at the time with the widespread doubt that women possessed an ability to reason, or even a soul.

Elizabeth had a complex character: 'cruel, capricious, insincere, at once unpleasantly masculine and weakly feminine'. She was better than an intelligent ruler: she had the rare and priceless instinct for picking the right men to tell her what to do. She was hugely popular with her subjects, for her image as much as for the satisfying national self-assertion of 'the times of Good Queen Bess'. She inherited Henry VIII's mastery of showbiz monarchy (the Field of the Cloth of Gold was his great production, if the *Mary Rose's* ceremonious sailing from Portsmouth was a flop), and her rousing speeches were scripted as skilfully as Churchill's. 'An element of lovemaking in diplomacy was always very much to her taste,' noticed Walsingham.

She had a small mouth, a flat nose, bad teeth and an ulcer on her leg like her father. She had continual imaginary illnesses but reached the exceptional age of seventy, when she had long shunned looking at herself in a glass, painted her face and put vermilion on her nose, and at night crankily plunged a rusty sword into her bedroom hangings for fear of lurkers.

She died at Richmond on 24 March 1603. According to Mrs Stone's *Chronicles of Fashion* in 1845:

> Queen Elizabeth left behind her a wardrobe containing three thousand dresses. Three years before her death, her wardrobe, *exclusive* of her coronation, mourning, parliament robes, and those of the Order of the Garter, consisted of:

99 Robes
102 French gownes
67 Rounde gownes
100 Loose gownes
126 Kirtells (*skirts*)
136 Forepartes (*ornamental breast coverings*)
125 Petticoates
96 Cloakes
31 Cloakes and saufegardes (*riding-skirts*)
13 Saufgardes
43 Saufegardes and juppes (*bodices*)
85 Dublettes
18 Lappe mantles
27 Fannes
9 Pantobles (*slippers*)

A royally sexual dresser.

She was not just a technical virgin. She menstruated irregularly and seldom. It was around all the ambassadors at court that she was unable to have children, or even to copulate. 'That she had a membrana on her which made her incapable of man, though for her delight she tried many,' revealed Ben Jonson. 'Ther was a French Chirurgion who took in hand to cut it, yett fear stayed her & his death.'

She suffered from a vaginal opening congenitally narrow, or from vaginismus, a reflex contraction of the pelvic muscles which renders penetration difficult or impossible, of psychological origin. Professor Freud would have begun his case-notes with her father beheading her mother when she was aged two, and her stepmother Catherine when she was eight.

'I hate the idea of marriage, for reasons that I would not divulge to a twin soul,' Elizabeth once confided in the Duke of Sussex. Less intimately she said: 'I would rather be a beggar and single than a queen and married.' An earnestly matchmaking House of Commons she snubbed: 'I am already bound unto a husband which is the Kingdom of England.' But the House of Commons did not get the implication. The political triumph of Elizabeth was making her virginity a national asset.

FOUR

A Sexual Empire

When I was thirteen, we left Germany for China. I remember
every stop we made on the *Haruna Maru* – Port Said, Suez,
Aden, Bombay, Colombo, Singapore, Hong Kong, and
Shanghai. And at every stop the Union Jack was flying
and a British officer in knee socks, with a topee and a swagger
stick, would come aboard and say, 'Howjado'. So now the
British are gone . . .

> Former Secretary of the US Treasury, Michael Blumenthal,

> 1978

Yo-ho-ho, and a Nice Cup of Tea!

We British are a ridiculous nation of cheerful pirates.
Geography left us no choice. Rival nations in Europe
could march casually across one another's frontiers, but
invading Britain was a troublesome operation involving
boats, tides, weather, shoals, sands, seasickness and the
ability to swim. Between William the Conqueror's successful Operation Hastings in 1066 and Hitler's scratched
Operation Sealion in 1940, the enemies of Britain made
mostly unhappy landings.

The landbound Continentals none the less looked
speculatively over their shoulders at the ocean. Spain
sailed off to take most of South America, Portugal had
Brazil, France collected Canada and bits of India, the
Dutch got the veldt and New York. But the British, who

felt the sea spray in their faces from all directions, searched the watery horizons more astutely. It was simpler to let others take the trouble of exploration, colonisation and exploitation, and then to seize the products.

The Spanish had forged a gold and silver ring across the Atlantic which sparkled invitingly in the eyes of Drake, the pirate king. He hijacked Spanish mule trains loaded with Peru silver crossing the Panama Isthmus to the Atlantic (£40,000 loot), and he plundered Valparaiso on his way home around the world aboard the *Golden Hind*. The Spanish were so furious at English ships invading the hemisphere specifically given to them by Pope Alexander VI, that Queen Elizabeth diplomatically hesitated for six months before creating him Sir Francis on deck at Deptford on 4 April 1581.

Among the memorable members of the pirate crew was Martin Frobisher, a wild, unlettered lad from Yorkshire, who left his name on icy Frobisher Bay in Baffin Island, where in 1576 he excitedly loaded up with gold ore – which was found to contain no gold, and the lumps were used to pave the English roads. Thomas Dover was a bad-tempered Bristol physician, who in 1708 pirated the Spaniards in the South Seas so successfully that he moved to a more fashionable practice in London, where he prescribed metallic mercury so lavishly, whatever his patients' diseases, he became even richer as 'the Quicksilver Doctor'. Welshman Bartholomew Roberts, killed in 1722, captor of 400 ships, was a teetotal pirate who forbade women and gambling aboard, a strict Sabbatarian who captured a clergyman so that he might sail with a ship's chaplain.

Anne Bonny and Mary Read were piratical feminists. Anne was born in Cork, the illegitimate daughter of a lawyer. She sailed with the pirate captain Rackam to Cuba, disguised as a man and unsuspected by all. In the East Indies, Anne became a shipmate of Mary, who also was disguised as a handsome young fellow. Anne fell in love with her and declared her sex. Whether this was the end, or the beginning, of a delightful relationship was not elaborated by Daniel Defoe, who told the story in 1726. Captain Rackam grew jealous, shortly all three were captured, and Anne chided him unmercifully on his execution morn: 'If you had fought like a man, you wouldn't find yourself hung like dog.' Both Anne and Mary avoided execution through pregnancy.

The invigorating draughts of money and patronage which sustained Britain's salty – or dusty – buccaneers were sugared with sexual urges. Some men sailed in the wind of religious passion, to find a home for undefiled Puritanism: but many others dispersed across the world from Hudson Bay to Calcutta to escape Puritanical repressions. The adventurers enjoyed comfortable neglect by a homeland preoccupied with civil and European war, and discovered themselves cheerfully loosed from the irritating conventions of British society. 'The scum of England' could later be poured into the useful colonies: in Australia, one in seven of the convicts transported to Botany Bay and to Port Arthur in Tasmania were women, half of these Irish, and they had only prostitution to work their passage home.

The haphazardly spread British Empire became brilliantly illuminated by Queen Victoria, Disraeli lighting the gas. The public-school Empire builder, who cut his sexual teeth on the ubiquitous servant girls (until the last quarter of the century, these had not taken to the spreading fashion of wearing knickers), once overseas was freed from middle-class prudery and found the world his succulent sexual oyster.

The tropical settler had his excuse of cruel isolation in the maddening midday sun and the sultry mosquito-buzzing nights. He could guiltlessly pirate sex from the natives who were eagerly waiting to surrender it to their

43

new masters. Also, the eastern prostitutes were far more genteel than the London sort, altogether cleaner, better dressed, more adept and more intelligent (particularly the well-travelled Japanese ones), and they could sing to you as well. If the colonist cared to exchange spasmodic variety for steady enjoyment of these attractive qualities, native mistresses afforded the supplementary usefulness of teaching their own language, and were gratefully named 'sleeping dictionaries'.

By 1913, a third of British exports and three-quarters of British emigrants went to the Empire. The red splashed across the atlas, denoting British rule, became a matter of unthinking complacency for British children learning geography. This cartography aroused the fierce jealousy of both Kaiser Wilhelm and Führer Hitler, for which the world suffered horrible violence spread across forty years. Hitler should have known better: 'No people has ever with greater brutality better prepared its economic conquests with the sword, and later ruthlessly defended them, than the English nation,' he wrote in *Mein Kampf*.

A national talent for piracy is hard to quell.

Sex Under the Raj

Drake's landlubber equivalent was Robert Clive, who, after the Black Hole of Calcutta in 1756 (123 died overnight out of 146 English prisoners sharing 18 feet by 15 feet), routed the local nabob at Plessy and set the English course to grab the French and Dutch acquisitions and to run India.

The populous peninsula a century later shone as the brightest jewel in the Imperial Crown. Queen Victoria was acclaimed its Empress in 1877, and her three succeeding monarchs wore as a halo to their heads on the duodecimal coinage: 'F. D. IND: IMP:' – *fidei defensor* and *India imperator*, Defender of the Faith and Emperor of India, two titles of equal significance and pride to their domestic people.

None of the Continental powers, who imposed themselves directly as rulers of their discovered lands, enjoyed such lasting success as colonisers as the British. We achieved this simply, by our constant behaviour as, and sincere belief in, being in every way superior humans to the natives.

Sex became an irritating complication in this governmental mechanism. A man's superiority is put in doubt when he has sexual intercourse with the native women, just like the native men do.

The most painful effect of this difficulty in India was felt by the British Army.

In 1890, the number of cases of venereal disease in the Army stationed in India was 438 per thousand; in 1896 it had risen to 522 per thousand. Of an infantry regiment paraded for colonel's inspection, almost half the men would have sore cocks. By 1902, the cases had fallen to 281 per thousand, by 1905 to 154 per thousand and by 1909 to 68 per thousand. In 1926, the rate had increased again to 110 (184 in Ceylon), while the Army based at home was suffering only 40 per thousand though regiments posted to China hit 333 per thousand. When the Navy sailed to India, it collected 204 cases per thousand going ashore.

Venereal disease then meant gonorrhoea and syphilis. The 'clap' brought scalding pee three or four days after infection, followed by a discharge of pus from the penis and tender lumps in the groin. With bad luck, this was followed by acute pain, swelling and tenderness in a testicle. The 'syph' meant a chancre (pronounced 'shanker') wherever the sexual intruder had hit the infec-

45

tion – it was usually on the penis, a small, hard painless ulcer which appeared a month afterwards. After a few more months, the patient developed the vague appearance of measles, with a sore throat, fever, lumps from infected lymph-glands everywhere, and a widespread rash the colour of raw ham, but non-irritating. Slimy greyish patches occurred in the mouth ('snail-track ulcers') and possibly warts round the anus. The patient became highly infective.

Before the sulphonamides and penicillin arrived to relieve this military plight in World War Two, there was no effective treatment whatever. The clap had been known since 1879 to be caused by the gonococcus, bean-shaped germs clasping themselves in pairs. The patients got irrigation with silver nitrate, or later a pink solution of potassium permanganate, supplied under pressure from a raised tank through a nozzle inserted into the penis. The corkscrew-like spirochete causing syphilis was discovered in Hamburg in 1906, August von Wassermann's neat test for diagnosing the disease was invented in Berlin in 1909 and Paul Ehrlich of Frankfurt produced in 1909 his antisyphilitic 'magic bullet' of salvarsan, '606'. But this was an uncertain and toxic remedy, and anyway neither the test nor the cure impinged on the British Army in India.

The only offering to the malevolent spirit of syphilis was pirate-doctor Thomas Dover's quicksilver. Military syphilitics were rubbed with mercury ointment, or dosed with mercurous chloride (calomel), or given intramuscular mercury injections or a mercury vapour bath. 'For this purpose the patient sits on a chair, wrapped round with blankets, leaving the head exposed, and 60 grains of calomel are volatilised by a water-bath and spirit-lamp placed under the chair. The proceeding lasts fifteen or twenty minutes,' directed a 1904 textbook of medicine. It added discouragement to discomfort: 'During the use

46

of mercury the patient should abstain from smoking and from stimulants, and live in every way as healthy a life as possible.'

The after-effects made a sorry old soldier's tale.

The purulent penis of gonorrhoea cleared up in time, like a runny nose. But scars of the infection created fibrous bands constricting the urinary passage, necessitating its painful dilation in the years ahead with a curved metal staff slipped skilfully up the penis to the bladder. 'The method of passing a bougie or catheter can be much better learned by five minutes' practice than by any written instructions,' advises a 1903 surgery textbook. Hard luck on the operator's first patient. The gonorrhoea sufferer could develop also inflammation of the iris and of all the joints.

The chancre healed into a perpetually condemnatory penile scar. The secondary syphilitic rash faded. Twenty years later, the patient developed gumata, lumps appearing anywhere on his body and breaking down into ulcers. He may have faced angina and sudden death, if he got syphilitic bulging of the aorta which conveyed the blood from his heart. He may have got tabes, making him fall over his feet, and general paralysis of the insane, which incited such delusions of grandeur as the conviction of really being Field Marshal Kitchener. The venereal patients carried on soldiering, but the crippling and killing effects of tertiary syphilis attacked them after discharge from the Service. Such men with gonorrhoeal or syphilitic infection, caught in India before the discovery of antibiotics, still appeared in NHS hospitals in Britain in the 1950s as memorials to the Army's inability to handle the problem.

The main cause of the VD epidemic – which, had it been of the more pressingly lethal dysentery or cholera would have been energetically countered – was the thoughtful provision by the Army of regimental brothels.

47

Paying a native woman to copulate was of course no more an infringement of British superiority than paying her to clean your boots.

The East Kent Regiment, stationed towards the foot of the Himalayas at Bareilly in 1887, spread its neat lines of tents on one side of the main road; on the other was the soldiers' lavatory marquee, the Christian church and two more lines of tents comprising the regimental brothel. These *lal bazars* then furnished seventy-five military establishments from Peshawar by the Khyber Pass to Trichinopoly on the way to Ceylon. When the regiment moved, so did the camp-followers who did the washing and the tailoring and the sweeping, and the whores.

A soldier needed his commanding officer's permission to wed, which was sparingly given because it put the Army to the expense and inconvenience of providing married quarters. Privates faced a marriage quota of 12 per cent, recorded in 1862 as only half fulfilled because colonels thought anyway that unmarried soldiers were more effective. And privates had this propensity for marrying native women, to be forcefully discouraged as ludicrously, but dangerously, indicating that the man and wife might be one flesh. (Though Kipling later suggested we conveniently colonised Kashmir by marrying off discharged soldiers to the locals.) Nor were officers privileged: married allowances were paid only after thirty, so that only promotion to major effectively brought the possibility of married bliss.

Privates had nothing much to do all day except loafing round the barracks. Regimental cricket and cross-country running, the Army Bureau of Current Affairs, the Entertainments National Services Association (ENSA, 'Every Night Something Awful') were unimagined competitors for sex and drinking in their leisure time. Though by 1897 the Army was considering organis-

48

ing some sort of athletic diversion, hoping to wear out the sportsmen 'as a deterrent to sexual indulgence'.

Overshadowing all was the horrible monster of homosexuality, which, from contemporary literature, was persecuted and performed equally passionately. Chief Empire builder Rhodes and Chief Boy Scout Baden-Powell were probably homosexual, but that made no excuse for anyone. One painstaking Army officer secretly listed 129 native boy partners, each undergoing an average of 12.3 orgasms, between Queen Victoria's Diamond Jubilee and the Russian Revolution. Across the Indian Ocean in Uganda, in 1885 thirty-one young men and boys were burnt alive for homosexuality, a punishment attracting encouragement from the missionaries. Even the uninfectious alternative of masturbation was worrying, because it sent you mad. The authorities could only grieve that the British private lacked the ability to rise above sexual temptation as a service to his country, a quality assumed to be at the ready disposal of the superior social classes.

The Army's thoughtful provision for its rankers attracted criticism. As well as restless sea-dogs Britain produced zestful sky-pilots, missionaries who would slight the morals of the rulers, as readily as of the ruled, whom it was their occupation to convert. This was thought unsporting, the British seeing the missionaries as living indications of the unquestionable superiority of the rulers' morals, as of everything else. The outbreaks of endemic morality at home reached across the seas to spoil the fun: Josephine Butler's Purity Campaign achieved in 1888 the suspension in India of the Contagious Diseases Act, which after 1864 had compelled the registration and medical examination of prostitutes gathered round the garrisons and docks of Britain. The fury of the moralist 'puritywallahs' at any state regulation of prostitution unfortunately blinded them to abolishing the only measure that was reducing its evil effects. Florence Nightingale characteristically perceived this in 1897.

The regimental 'rag' was open from noon to eleven at night, the girls ran from prepubertal to the postmenopausal, the supply was about one girl per fifty available customers, and the cost in 1890 was sergeants one rupee (2s), corporals half that – eight annas – and four annas (6d) for privates. The girls were probably all infected with gonorrhoea or syphilis, some with both. Catching the disease from them was not inevitable, but it was a copulatory Russian roulette. In 1887, the Quartermaster-General dutifully reported refurnishing the *lal bazars* with 'a more attractive lot of women' who might be free from VD: but the newcomers caught it, and the most attractive of all were followed after their subsequent expulsion from the brothel by their enthusiastic customers. Perhaps this was worthy: recklessness in the face of danger is a cherished military quality.

The regimental brothel can shed some of the pestilential blame. If the *lal bazar* was monotonous or expensive, there were girls galore in the streets. In 1867, a calculated 30,000 prostitutes paraded in Calcutta (there were 80,000 in London). Grant Road, Bombay, was already a location smirkingly familiar to seafarers across the oceans of the world. In 1880, brothel registration was enforced in Calcutta, revealing 2,458 keepers and 7,001 prostitutes, but another 20,000 there were on the loose. In 1900, there were 40,000 female prostitutes in Shanghai, 800 boy prostitutes in Tientsin, and in Constantinople more male prostitutes than female ones. By 1930, Hong Kong had 2,600 registered brothels and Japan could count exactly 50,056 prostitutes.

If you were unhappily obliged to report to the regimental medical officer, you were treated at one of the Lock Hospitals which had been established in India since

1805. These hospitals had evolved from a lazar house beside the Thames, the first to welcome VD patients. The name may be derived from the old French *logues*, meaning bandages, or from the low English 'lock' meaning the female pudendum, to which men held the key. Lock Hospitals served encouragingly, but futilely, to treat the untreatable. Infected girls were sent there by the Indian *kotwal* in charge of the *lal bazar*, but probably returned to work still infective. Hyderabad in 1844 offered more personal treatment by an Indian matron, for which it taxed its prostitutes two annas a month, but dropped the scheme because bribery bought 'cure' and back to business.

Before the effective antibiotics, venereal infection could have been trivialised in the Army in India had the condom been a word and an article in as unashamed use as today. Condoms were familiar in the middle of the eighteenth century to James Boswell and to Casanova, who blew them up and patted them round the bedroom like balloons, sending his girl-friends into shrieks. But as 'French letters', or 'FLs', or 'Freddies' before reverting to their eighteenth-century name of condom – which sounds like an item of kitchen equipment – they never wildly caught on. They were embarrassing items of courtship which civilians bought discreetly at the barber's or stealthily at the chemist's.

In 1934, 400,000 condoms a week were being manufactured in Britain – which, the unmarried Bishop of London informed the House of Lords, he wished to make a bonfire of and dance round – a minute supply to furnish the copulation of an Empire. And the cost! A stout condom of vulcanised rubber in 1860 cost 10d, in the 1930s the 'packet of three', for which the newly smartened-up customers asked their barbers on leaving, demanded more than a pint of beer per act of love. No wonder the War

51

Office counted the cost as thoughtfully as the unenlisted youth of the country who had to buy its own safety.

In both world wars, the medical officers pressed condoms on their potential patients, with half-hearted official encouragement. The Catholic Church's horror of contraceptives ruthlessly spread a human misery and danger which it should have been proud to have culled. But the dominant cause of the condom's flop were easygoing youngsters who, before the AIDS terror, took VD as a hazard not worth such fussiness and diminution of pleasure. 'Washing your feet with your boots on' was the famous condemnatory phrase. It was countered by a medical brigadier before the Battle of El Alamein, who declared: 'Some of you fellows put your private parts where I wouldn't stick the ferrule of my umbrella.'

The Memsahib

The British with Indian mistresses presented the additional problem of bulk. A Christian man might have no wife and enjoy countless prostitutes, or he might faithfully cherish one wife, but mistresses multiplied limitlessly. The British Resident of Delhi in 1825 had thirteen. The Scots-Punjabi Colonel Skinner, commanding the famous Skinner's Horse, had fourteen mistresses (though his family protested after his death there were only seven) and eighty children. Job Charnock of the East India Company, the founder of Calcutta, acquired one mistress by bravely dragging her smouldering from *suttee* – the exemplary burning from which Hindu widows were indebted to Governor-General Lord William Bentick for sparing them after 1828.

At the end of the eighteenth century, a British official with such a *bibi* evoked not a second censorious thought.

After the Indian Mutiny was extinguished in 1857, the perilous frontier between intruder and inhabitants clearly needed the more vigilantly to be guarded. In 1900, there were 170,000 Europeans, to hypnotise into submission by their superiority 294 million Indians. A native mistress was a betrayal which could 'annihilate the respect paid to the British character, and ruin our Indian empire' – so feared the Colonial Office, issuing a circular to the entire Empire about it in 1909. This had a space for reply, inviting Governors to sneak on fellow officials having immoral relations with the natives, but in admirable public-school spirit none did.

Even English barmaids were bursting with danger. 'Incidents occur which are profoundly degrading to the prestige of the ruling race,' shuddered the 'most superior person' Viceroy Lord Curzon in 1902. There were thirty-six barmaids serving drinks in Rangoon, and a few in Calcutta 'to tempt in the young English clerks, and persuade the latter to spend their substance in drinking and frivolity, if not worse'. But the horror lay in their humiliatingly pouring pints for the natives. Curzon was obsessed about interracial sex, even in reverse among the grand Indian princes. The Maharaja of Patiala had married a Miss Florry Bryan in 1893, infuriatingly surmounting a former Viceroy's obstruction; when the Raja of Jind married Olive, whose German mother was in 1900 an exhibition parachutist to an American balloonist, Curzon was appalled. He had stopped one young raja attending Queen Victoria's Diamond Jubilee, from the danger that he might marry an Englishwoman. He had stopped another visiting France, from the danger of his copulating with a Frenchwoman, but the raja enjoyed an audience with the French President instead.

A native mistress meant blocked promotion and transfer to a bleaker posting; though Lord Curzon accepted the possibility of purification 'by a course of wholesome living'. Nobody bothered to reflect that a native mistress or wife provided the ruler with invaluable knowledge of the ruled, and that they were always excellent house-keepers. Curzon was equally prepared loftily to unbend towards the native dancers, nautch girls, who the purity-wallahs suggested made rude gestures in their act: 'The Viceroy . . . hardly thinks the matter is one upon which he is called upon to make any pronouncement or to take any action.' Curzon was so conscientious a Viceroy that he banned 'Onward Christian Soldiers' from the 1903 Durbar hymns because the lines:

> Crowns and Thrones may perish,
> Kingdoms rise and wane,

he considered a bit near the bone.

The Suez Canal was started in 1859 and opened in 1869, and soon sexual relief was arriving regularly by P & O steamers at Bombay. India no longer spelt exile. Wives, both acquired or potential, could be shipped inex-pensively from home, children dispatched punctually to the English public schools, expectant mothers comfort-ably floated off to Harley Street. (Englishwomen must be spared contact with Indian or Eurasian doctors, their gentlemen decided firmly, though the ladies themselves did not seem to mind.) Home leave became even more convenient, after disembarkment at Marseilles and taking the train to avoid the Bay of Biscay. Every year, when the Indian sun comfortably cooled, the famed 'fishing fleet' of unmarried Englishwomen were outward bound to hook the husbands that were beyond their powers of luring at home.

The *memsahib* had arrived down the P & O gangway. The British, as always, lived in Britain wherever they were, 'eating salmon from Scotland, and sardines from the Mediterranean, and observing that St Cloup's *potage à la Julienne* was perhaps better than his other soups, and that some of the ladies' sleeves were too tight', sighed Indian diarist Emily Eden. The effect of officials' wives in India was the formation of exclusive social groups in every British community, revolving round drinks and dinner parties, bridge, gossip, constant flirtations and infrequent adultery, and with no regard for, or interest in, anyone beyond their circumference. The *memsahib* steadily extended her rule, which was invaluable to the Raj for providing a genteel structure of life in a land which was irrefutably baffling and frightening. This was like life in a better-class London suburb: the Empire was laudably ruled by Surbiton and Slough, which, however uninspiring, were unlikely to exude cruel oppression upon anybody.

Mr Pooter's *Diary of a Nobody* appeared in 1892. Had he changed his job as City clerk for Empire builder, he would inevitably have become a Somebody. Leaving The Laurels, Holloway, for a verandahed bungalow in Cawnpore, Carrie Pooter would have at her light-fingered command a *dhobi wallah* to do the washing, *punka wallahs* to keep her cool, an *ayah* to nursemaid young Lupin, a *dhurzi* to tailor Mr Pooter's linen suits, sweepers from the untouchable caste to clean the lavatories, perhaps an esteemed Goanese cook and a turbaned butler to order the household about. *Pukka sahib* Charles Pooter, reaching home wearing his *sola topi* and flicking his fly-whisk, weary from commanding the *babu* clerks, had but to clap his hands and shout 'Boy!' to be brought obsequiously his sundowner *burra peg*, the *mem* possibly joining him with a smaller *chota peg* before they changed for dinner. The grander *memsahib* of the *burra sahibs* within the spread of viceregal glory could live and entertain with the careless abundance of Trollope's Duchess of Omnium.

If the British never invited Indians to their homes or to their clubs, nor shared with them their hospital wards or their railway compartments, nobody thought twice about an established and seemingly natural order of things. This life in India continued tranquilly until 1939. Who can blame its voluptuaries for imagining that it would go on for ever?

FIVE

Sweethearts and Wives

....

In the turbulent turn of the eighteenth century, its three glorious warriors impressed their personalities on women as idiosyncratically as upon the battlefields and seas of Europe.

Vive l'Empereur!

The twenty-first of November 1787 was a freezing Wednesday night in Paris. Napoleon the Corsican was staying at the Hôtel de Cherbourg off the rue Saint-Honoré, on the right bank of the Seine near the church of St Eustache, the miniature Notre Dame with a communal oven beside it. He decided on a brisk walk in the lanes round the Palais Royal, which now faces, across the rue de Rivoli, the Court Napoleon of the Louvre with its odd see-through Pyramid. His soul, stirred by its characteristic vigour, allowed him to bear the cold with indifference – so he wrote afterwards. But the winter bleakness drew him towards the galleries, which were brightly lit and warm, and where the fun was. He was eighteen, a second lieutenant in the artillery, poor and lonely.

At the iron entrance gates his glance fell upon a woman.

The hour, her figure, her extreme youth, left me in no doubt that she was a prostitute [he recorded in his diary]. I stared at her; she stopped, not with a toffee-nosed look, but with one perfectly matching the allure of her person. There was something between us. Her bashfulness encouraged me, and I spoke to her. I spoke to her! Me, who, more conscious than anyone of the obnoxiousness of her calling, has always felt soiled by a single glance from a whore . . . But her pale face, her frail body, her soft voice, did not allow me a moment's hesitation. I told myself, here's someone who will be useful to me in the observations that I wish to make – either that, or she is only a dimwit.

'You must be frightfully cold,' I said to her. 'How can you bring yourself to go wandering round the lanes?'

'Ah! Monsieur, it's hope that keeps me going. I've got to finish my evening's work.'

The casualness with which she pronounced these words, the phlegm of this reply, intrigued me, and I walked along with her.

'You seem of a somewhat feeble constitution. I'm amazed that your job doesn't wear you out.'

'You're right, monsieur, but a girl's got to do something.'

'Perhaps. But it's an occupation hardly beneficial to your health.'

'No, it isn't, monsieur, but a girl's got to live.'

I was enchanted. I felt that she at least responded to me, a success which had not crowned all the approaches which I had made to women.

'You must come from somewhere up north, as you can stand the cold?'

'I'm from Nantes, in Brittany.'

'I know that part of the world . . . Would you have the kindness, mademoiselle, of telling me how you lost your virginity?'

'An officer had me.'

'Are you cross about it?'

'Oh! Yes, believe you me.' (Her voice took an edge, a fervency that I hadn't noticed before.) 'I'll say so! My sister's well set up at the moment. Why aren't I?'

'Why did you come to Paris?'

'The officer who had me, who I hate, abandoned me. I had to get away from my mother's carrying on about it. A second feller turned up, took me to Paris, abandoned me, and a third, who I've lived with for three years, took over from him. He's French, but he had to go on a business trip to London. Let's go back to your place.'

'But what should we do?'

'Well, we can warm ourselves up, and I'll perform for your pleasure.'

I was far from being scrupulous; I had led her on, so that she could not save herself from falling for the line which I had taken, in feigning an honesty which I now wished to prove to her that I did not have . . .

So the conqueror of Europe was conquered by an amiable tart.

The old hypocrite.

When Napoleon was twenty-five and a brigadier, he met the two daughters of a millionaire in Marseilles. He fell for the younger, sixteen-year-old Désirée, a large-eyed, strong-jawed brunette, who, like Hitler's first love Gili, was a promising singer. Napoleon disliked her name and called her Eugénie, and put her in a short story he was writing. (Had Napoleon decided that the pen was mightier than the sword, it would have afforded him an estimable career and Europe less trouble. He had an inspiring style for his proclamations and orders, and a fingertip touch with an epigram: e.g., love was *une sottise faite à deux*, much as Chamfort had found it *l'échange de deux fantasies et le contact de deux épidermes*.)

Napoleon's penniless brother Joseph married the

millionaire's elder girl, Julie (dowry, a hundred thousand livres). Napoleon himself went to fight the Austrians and, like Hitler (a diabolically more interesting tyrant), became horrified at the notion of a woman interfering with his work. He wrote to Désirée, telling her as much. A year later, Napoleon changed his mind and decided that he would like to marry Désirée after all, but by then her mother had decided that one Bonaparte in the family was enough. Désirée became instead the Queen of Sweden.

In the autumn of 1795, Napoleon was twenty-six, in Paris on half pay and meeting prosaic women at unremarkable parties, when he encountered thirty-two-year-old Rose. She had been brought up in Martinique, where the family grew sugar and fermented rum upon the labour of a hundred and fifty slaves, but Martinique was now held by the English and she was broke. Rose was five feet tall, chestnut-haired, sharp-nosed, not beautiful but good-natured, sexually easygoing, living on her wits, an enthusiast for the occult, who eagerly told Napoleon's fortune. She had married a Viscomte but they had separated before his inevitable beheading in the Revolution, she had two children and she was the mistress of the Comte de Barras. The Comte was the overthrower of Robespierre, one of the five-man *Directoire* ruling France in their gorgeous plumed hats, a friend of Napoleon, who that 5 October saved his skin with Carlyle's 'whiff of grapeshot'.

Napoleon fell for Rose, but he disliked her name and changed it to Joséphine. He conducted their affair with his usual battlefield briskness. Next January he charged, and victoriously copulated. At seven the following morning he was writing passionately that: 'My mind is full of thoughts of you when I awake. Your picture and the memory of yesterday's intoxicating evening have left me in turmoil'; and that he drew from her lips and heart a flame which burnt him, adding – sexually complimentarily – that the idea which he had formed of her was quite different from the real Joséphine. 'What is your strange power, incomparable Joséphine?' he puzzled, resolving to marry her. Joséphine found him rough and randy and altogether odd, but tepidly took to the idea. The Comte de Barras was delighted, wishing to be rid of her, and promised Napoleon as a wedding present command of the Army of Italy.

The two citizens were married in the rue d'Antin by a registrar with a wooden leg on 9 March 1796. As both their homelands had been seized by the English, they used their siblings' birth certificates, which reduced the age gap. Napoleon discovered that he had to share his bride's bed with her pug dog, which bit him in the leg. Two days later, Napoleon abandoned his honeymoon for his headquarters in Nice, and on 15 May returned Barras thanks for his wedding present by triumphantly entering Milan, from where he promptly dispatched all movable works of art to Paris.

Napoleon was besotted with Joséphine. He kissed her portrait every hour: she left his in the drawer. He sent her a letter every day: she, once a week. She wrote to him as *vous*. '*Vous vous-même!*' responded Napoleon furiously. An oddity was shown in one of his letters: 'I'm coming tomorrow, don't wash.' Perhaps like Edward VII, who on summer afternoons sent his ladies out for a walk beforehand, he liked them slightly sweaty. It was a marriage of inconvenience. Napoleon's family thought she was tarty. But a century later Englishmen who waggishly quoted 'Not tonight, Joséphine!' were as blithely misinformed as the Frenchman who described them as a nation of shopkeepers.

The eagerness of the London press to poke its nose into important bedrooms is long-standing. On Saturday 24 November 1798, the *Morning Chronicle* printed a letter from Napoleon in Egypt, which he had invaded as the preferential alternative to invading England. It was written to his brother Joseph at home, expressing his anguish at Joséphine's infidelity while she was taking the cure at Plombières-les-Bains, the spa in the Vosges. The lapse was incurred with the handsome Lieutenant Hippolyte Charles, a draper's son, who made jokes, which Napoleon did not. 'The veil has been horribly torn asunder,' were Napoleon's distraught words to amuse the English public, the impeccable source of the letter being its interception by Nelson.

Napoleon, who had been writing to Joséphine of his desire to strip from her body the last shred of chiffon, consoled himself in Cairo by doing as much with Pauline, the blonde wife of one of his lieutenants, who had come out to help with the army laundry. On St Helena, he reminisced about his women as Hitler did one evening during his own war, but Napoleon more efficiently captured seven of them.

In Paris, among the ladies of his court who became his sexual aides-de-camp shone one perpetuated as Madame ***. She was twenty, with a husband of fifty, charming and pretty, but with a long nose. Displaying as usual *la rapidité*, Napoleon fell for her in November 1803 and on 5 August 1804 she gave him a baby. Joséphine objected to the relationship. During a reception at St-Cloud, Napoleon talked to all the women guests so that he might talk alone to Madame ***, creating the persistent and fatuous story of the olives.

As a dish of olives was placed before Madame ***, Napoleon warned: 'You're wrong to eat olives at night, they're bad for you.' Turning to her neighbour, he observed: 'And you don't eat olives? You're right, and doubly so in not imitating madame, because in everything she is inimitable.'

Next day, Joséphine asked this neighbour what Napoleon had said to Madame ***.

'He advised her not to eat olives in the evening.'

'H'm,' said Joséphine sniffily, 'when he gives such advice he should add that it's ridiculous to *faire la Roxelane* with such a long nose' – Roxelane being the favourite wife of the all-conquering Sultan Suleiman II the Magnificent of the mid-sixteenth century, who captured Belgrade and Rhodes and crushed the Magyars (I told you it was a piffling story).

Napoleon added to his sexual staff a contralto and an actress, Joséphine Weimar, who used Mademoiselle George as her stage name, which he predictably disliked and changed to Georgina. He invented for her some snappy elastic garters, and paid her off with 40,000 francs, presented by pushing them down her bosom. His conquest of Europe provided the pleasant incidental of a multinational selection of mistresses. In Warsaw, he selected at a ball twenty-year-old blonde Marie Walewska, wife of the rich Count Anastas Walewski, who was almost fifty years older than she. Displaying again the brisk efficiency with which he went to war, he dispatched next morning a fervent invitation and afterwards he copulated and corresponded with her with equal passion. In 1810 she gave him a son, Alexandre Walewski, about whom he was fussy and bossy. Napoleon also cheated at chess.

Napoleon rose at six with a cup of tea, like Hitler always shaved himself, then spent an hour in the bath, topping up the hot water. In 1797, Madame de Staël, incomparable intellectual, called to see him at his house in Paris. His *valet de chambre* apologised that the Citizen General was in the bath-tub, stark naked. 'No matter!' cried Madame de Staël. 'Genius has no sex!' Napoleon did not think this funny.

Germaine de Staël had been the mistress of Talleyrand

(after their break-up she portrayed him in a vengeful novel as a Madame de Vernon: 'I understand that madame de Staël, in her novel has disguised both herself and me as women,' he observed). She was enjoying a tempestuous relationship with Benjamin Constant (who spectacularly attempted suicide with opium on her behalf in 1795, but safely with a homeopathic dose). She saw Napoleon as the foremost man in the world; she was the foremost woman; they must mate; *c'est logique.* 'Who is the greatest woman, alive or dead?' she asked him invitingly at a dinner party. 'The one who has made the most children,' he told her, with Hitlerian fundamentalism.

Germaine was thirty-one, fat, full-lipped, big-eyed, plain and rompish; she went about twiddling a sprig of poplar and she shouted a lot. She had resided for a while between Leatherhead and Dorking. Her *salon* in Paris was esteemed a fermenting intellectual vat, from which her ideas bubbled away brilliantly into the fresh, post-Revolutionary air. Her pursuit of Napoleon was ludicrous. She could not grasp that even a military and political genius prefers women who are ordinary. She sighed over him: 'From his earliest years he has coveted power; before his mind was formed, artifice took hold of it and estranged the nascent voice of nature.' He was a cold calculator, she was the warm champion of the human race, which was advancing through scientific progress towards moral perfection. That sad contrariety she saw as their trouble.

In 1803, Napoleon exiled Germaine from Paris, and she went to Weimar to dazzle Schiller and Goethe. 'He fears me. That is my joy, my pride and my terror,' she exclaimed, with habitual exhibitionism and consoling self-delusion. It mystifies intellectual women, who generally take themselves with befitting seriousness, that men respond to their concomitant longing for affection by finding them undisguisedly a pain in the arse. Napoleon anyway expected writers, like generals, to obey his orders, and quashed free speech in pulpit or press. He instructed Germaine's Benjamin Constant: 'I don't hate liberty. I clear it out of the way, when it's obstructing my route' – epigrammatical in his tyranny.

Joséphine had become infertile: perhaps she had suffered a pelvic infection. Napoleon's sperm count seemingly passed muster, though a British doctor noticed when he was safely dead:

> Indeed the whole body was slender and effeminate.
> There was scarcely any hair on the body and that
> of the head was thin, fine and silky. The pubis much
> resembled the Mons Veneris in Women. The
> muscles of the chest were small, the shoulders were
> narrow and the hips wide.

By the summer of 1807, Napoleon ran a one-man European Union with more efficiency and less argument than achieved by Brussels 186 years later. France, Benelux, Italy, Spain, Portugal and Germany were ruled by directives from Napoleon's quill, all conceived to benefit their inhabitants by orientating them towards the standard of civilisation expressed by France. England remained awkwardly Eurosceptic. Recalling that 'The wooden walls are the best walls of this kingdom', England expressed her objections by seizing the Danish fleet and landing on the Peninsula.

Napoleon was rising forty, and needed a legitimate heir. He was fond of Joséphine, but she would have to go, like an unlucky general. Also, she was devilishly extravagant, ten pairs of shoes a week, forty hats a year, *c'est ridicule*. There was a door between their bedrooms, as between Hitler's and his mistress Eva Braun's, and

Napoleon's having it bricked up seemed an adequate hint of impending marital annulment.

On 15 November 1809 the marriage pronounced by the one-legged registrar, later solemnised hastily and privately the night before Napoleon's coronation as Emperor on 2 December 1804, was scratched and Joséphine left with her dogs. Napoleon decided to procreate with Anna, the fifteen-year-old sister of Tsar Alexander I. He had met Alexander aged twenty-nine on a raft in the middle of the River Niemen, and had thought that, had the Tsar been a woman, he would have fallen passionately in love with him (the Napoleonic view of homosexuals – one was his High Chancellor the Duke of Parma – was exemplarily of resigned toleration).

Napoleon recommended the match between himself and Anna as having the incidental joy of cementing the peace of Europe. But her grandmother wouldn't let her. So in 1810 Napoleon married instead the eighteen-year-old daughter of the Emperor of Austria.

The Archduchess Marie-Louise was a blue-eyed brunette, who he recalled in St Helena liked it twice a night. After the marriage, Napoleon both learned to waltz and began to put on weight. A year later, Marie-Louise dutifully bore him by forceps delivery a son, who became the King of Rome and died aged twenty-one from tuberculosis. Marie-Louise did not join him on Elba four years later, but Marie Walewska came for a couple of days, bringing *that* son. Marie Walewska had called on him in the pit of despair, abandoned by all at Fontainebleau in February 1814. She spent the night in an antechamber, but had left before Napoleon, absorbed in thought, summoned her. 'The poor woman! She believes herself forgotten,' he sighed after her. That May, Joséphine died at Malmaison from diphtheria, her hair still forming Napoleon's watch-chain.

After Waterloo, England could not decide whether to

send Napoleon to Scotland or to the Azores or to hang him, but chose St Helena, conveniently owned by the East India Company.

Nobody in St Helena knew that he was coming. Nobody had heard of Waterloo or Elba. Napoleon went ashore from the seventy-eight-gun *Northumberland* on 15 October 1815 and put up at the local pub. He was installed at Longwood House, which was single-storey, wooden, with a billiard-room and a barn and a cowshed, isolated in the mud like an English farmhouse. This did not mitigate his disappointment at his destination, Napoleon having confidently expected to end his life as an English country gentleman.

Napoleon had for comfort neither his favourite wife nor his favourite mistress. Marie-Louise stayed in Vienna, and in the style of unhappy princesses sought sympathy and then sex from one of her compliant courtiers, Count Neipperg. Marie Walewska's husband died in 1814, and two years later at Liège she married a cousin of Napoleon's, one of his glittering officers in *la Grande Armée*, the General Comte d'Ornano. The marriage deeply affected Napoleon; one of his entourage wrote of his constant extreme tenderness for her, adding that it was not in his nature to allow one whom he loved to love anything else but himself. Marie became ill in the summer of 1817, and died in Paris in December just as her hurrying husband reached her hotel in the rue de la Victoire. Napoleon desired in his will that his son Alexandre enter the service of the French Army, but he did better and became foreign minister to Napoleon III.

Napoleon at St Helena was allowed twelve servants and three aides-de-camp, from whom, and a handful of ultimate friends and their wives, he created a sad little court. *Chez lui* he was the Emperor, but he was General Bonaparte to the British, who posted sentries under the windows at night. Dinner was ceremoniously announced by the silk-breeched butler at eight, but it was the British who controlled the wine consumption.

He died on 5 May 1821, from a perforated peptic ulcer (my own diagnosis) or from a carcinoma of the stomach (his Corsican doctor's). Or he was killed by his wallpaper. In 1978, chemists at Glasgow University found a lock of his hair to contain sixty times the normal arsenic level, and in 1980 a chemist in Newcastle-upon-Tyne discovered a scrap of the green, rosette-patterned flock wallpaper torn as a souvenir from his bedroom at St Helena. This emitted arsenic vapour when damp – and Longwood was dripping damp, like an English farmhouse – at a strength ten times that recorded for twenty cases of wallpaper poisoning discovered in St Louis in 1893. As the scientists chuckled, Was the murderer hung before the victim died? The post-mortem was performed in the billiard-room. Napoleon gave his heart literally to Marie-Louise, but a British doctor left it overnight in a washbasin, and the rats ate it. Napoleon's dental implements, gold scrapers and probes in a box bearing his arms, were sold at Christie's in 1994 for £62,000.

Napoleon was methodical in planning, adaptable in battle, ruthless with his soldiers' lives, and had good guns. The massive monumental commemorations of his triumphs record easy enemies. He had never faced Wellington before the morning of Waterloo, having prudently avoided the running sore in Spain. He was more realistic sexually and politically than Hitler. 'Everything I say and do is history,' asserted Hitler. Napoleon more modestly asked: 'What will they say of me when I am gone?' and replied: 'They will say "*Ouf*".'

Love letter from Napoleon to Joséphine, from Paris, 1795:

> You are leaving at noon; I shall see you in three
> hours. Until then, mio dolce amor, a thousand
> kisses; but give me none in return, for they set my
> blood on fire.

Love letter from Nelson to Lady Hamilton, from HMS
Medusa, 1801:

> I am so dreadfully seasick, that I cannot hold up
> my head!

Love letter from Napoleon to Joséphine, from Nice, 1796:

> I have not spent a day without loving you; I have
> not spent a night without embracing you; I have
> not so much as drunk a single cup of tea without
> cursing the pride and ambition which force me to
> remain separated from the moving spirit of my life.
> In the midst of my duties, whether I am at the head
> of my army or inspecting the camps, my beloved
> Joséphine stands alone in my heart, occupies my
> mind, fills my thoughts . . . The day when you say
> 'I love you less' will mark the end of my love and
> the last day of my life. If my heart were base enough
> to love without being loved in return I would tear
> it to pieces. Joséphine! Joséphine! Remember what
> I have sometimes said to you: Nature has endowed
> me with a virile and decisive character. It has built
> yours out of lace and gossamer.

Love letters from Nelson to Lady Hamilton, from HMS
Amazon, 1801:

> I am, in truth, not over well. I have a complaint in
> my stomach and bowels but it will go off. If you
> was here, I should have some rhubarb; but as you are

not, I shall go without. Sutton has sent into
Yorkshire, for a cow that, in the spring, will give
fourteen pounds of butter a week; and, he has given
Allen the finest goat I ever saw. The latter, I am
afraid, will be troublesome.

The cold has settled in my bowels. I wish the
Admiralty had my complaint; but, they have no
bowels; at least for me.

From HMS *Victory*, 1805:

I have had, about four o'clock this morning, one of
my dreadful spasms, which has almost enervated me.
It is very odd! I was hardly ever better than
yesterday . . . However, it is entirely gone off, and
I am only quite weak. The good people of England
will not believe, that rest of body and mind is
necessary for me! But, perhaps, this spasm may not
come on again those six months . . . I joined the
fleet late on the evening of 28th of September, but
could not communicate with them until the next
morning. I believe, my arrival was most welcome;
not only to the commander of the fleet, but also
to every individual in it; and, when I came to
explain to them the *Nelson touch*, it was like an
electric shock.

MY DEAREST BELOVED EMMA AND THE DEAR
FRIEND OF MY BOSOM, – The signal has been
made that the enemy's combined fleet are coming
out of port. We have very little wind, so that I have
no hope of seeing them before to-morrow. May the
God of Battles crown my endeavours with
success! . . . and as my last writing before the battle
will be to you, so I hope in God that I shall live
to finish my letter after the battle.

October 20th in the morning we were close to
the mouth of the Straights, but the wind had not
come far enough to the westward to allow the

combined fleets to weather the shoals of Trafalgar,
but they were counted as far as forty sail of ships
of war which I suppose to be 34 of the line, and six
frigates. A group of them was seen off the lighthouse
of Cadiz this morning, but it blows so very fresh,
that I rather believe they will go into harbour before
night. May God Almighty give us success over
these fellows and enable us to get a Peace!

This letter was found open in Nelson's desk after
Trafalgar.

The message of love can be adequately conveyed by
two initialled, arrow-pierced hearts carved on the trunk
of a tree. But the most powerful of human urges, specifically implanted by God to multiply the human race,
understandably incites a more elaborate expression. The
writers of love letters pant over their pens to impress
their receivers with the grandeur of their passion, or at
least with the trouble they have taken to express it. Love
letters and diaries became a fashionable intimate art in
the early seventeenth century, as more people became
literate and fell under the inspiration of Puritanism and
began searching their souls the more busily. Some wrote
to their loves to impress themselves smugly with their
works or, if they were pros at the writing game, later to
impress readers and critics with their published amorous
outpourings and to make a bit of money.

Some lovers correspond in the same style as they chat
across the fireside: to address the beloved all day in tones
of high literary passion would be swiftly boring and
exhausting for both. Napoleon wrote to Joséphine with
the professionalism he applied to his inspiring Orders
of the Day, but Nelson preferred a spontaneity which
reflected his successful style in both naval and sexual
strategy.

Nelson had two women, Fanny and Emma.

In the spring of 1785, the twenty-eight-gun *Boreas*, a

year out of Portsmouth, dropped anchor off Charlestown, the capital of Nevis, an insignificant island in the middle of the Leewards south of St Kitts, the tip of an extinct volcano poking from the Caribbean. Pausing only to seize four American merchant ships anchored in the roads, her commander, Nelson, went ashore for dinner with the President of Nevis, John Herbert, a widower whose niece, Fanny Nisbet, managed the domestic slavery.

Fanny was twenty-seven, the same age as Nelson, the widow of the doctor who had supervised her father's death, and she had a son. She was a dull-looking woman, but she could play the piano, sew and speak French; she was the passable wife of any passing naval officer. They married at Nevis on 11 March 1787, the bride given away by post-captain Prince William, to be the Sailor King. Fanny's attraction was reminding Nelson of Mary Moutray, whom he had earlier fancied in Antigua. Mary was seven years older than Nelson and thirty years younger than her husband, a jolly but disastrous captain who ran the Antigua dockyard. She was sharp-faced, witty, an ornament to any English drawing-room, but she had been obliged to take her sick husband home to Bath, where he died: had he died more felicitously in Antigua, Nelson would have taken her alongside instead.

In midwinter 1798 – he was now Lord Nelson and the victor of the Nile – Nelson was dispatched in the seventy-four-gun *Vanguard* to rescue the King and Queen of Naples from Napoleon's unstoppable army. King Ferdinand IV (*Nasone*, from his large nose) was expert at pig-sticking, shooting and fishing but could hardly read or write. His Queen, Maria Carolina, Marie Antoinette's sister, welcomed Nelson ardently. Her intimate friend was Emma, the wife of the British Ambassador, Sir William Hamilton – so intimate that the French sympathisers in Naples put it about that they were les. Emma sailed out of Naples in the welcoming fleet of small boats, climbed aboard *Vanguard*, cried 'Oh God, is it possible!' and fainted on deck at Nelson's feet.

Emma, christened Amy Lyon, a blacksmith's daughter from the Wirral (the genteel end of Liverpool) who matured in Flintshire, was then thirty-three. At sixteen, she had become nursemaid for Dr Richard Budd, a physician at St Bartholomew's Hospital in London. This seemed not her *métier*, for she found herself destitute and obliged to sell her healthy teeth for unanaesthetised extraction and their implantation, then fashionable, into someone's denuded gums. Her journey to the dentist was luckily intercepted by the naval captain who became Admiral Payne, who more naturally extracted from her a baby.

Emma next became a Goddess in the Temple of Health in Pall Mall, created by James Graham, the loudest quack in a flourishing flock. His miracle cures were performed in an excitable aura of flashing lights, leaping flames, Arabian perfumes and off-stage music. The Temple's speciality was its Celestial Bed, which had a mattress stuffed with stallion's tails, purple sheets, was tiltable in all desired directions and rested on three-quarters of a ton of magnets to attract fertility. It cost childless couples £100 a night, but included breakfast. Ex-medical student Graham delivered clinical lectures, holding his audience's attention with electric shocks delivered spasmodically through their seats, or more pleasantly by the 'female who was lectured upon, who had no more clothing than Venus when she rose from the sea'.

Emma was already recorded to have shown 'great talent' at family theatricals while a domestic servant, and offered the part of Goddess 'a perfect figure, fine regular features, and an indescribable charm and attractiveness about her face and expression'. Such recommended her in 1782 (when the Temple financially

73

collapsed) to be mistress of Sir Harry Fetherstonhaugh at Up Park in Sussex, who passed her on (as Emily Hart) to the Hon. Charles Greville, an MP with £500 a year who lived frugally at Paddington Green, who four years later passed her on to Sir William Hamilton, his uncle, for a testamentary consideration. George Romney meanwhile joined in these exchanges fervently but sexlessly, justifying himself by his painting Emma thirty times in roles from a Magdalene and a Bacchante to Joan of Arc, as well as 'naked Leda with a swan'.

Sir William Hamilton was fifty-six, ex-Foot Guards, the widower of a beautiful Pembrokeshire heiress, living on £5,000 a year. He was an antiquarian who in 1764 had himself conveniently appointed British Ambassador to Naples, where he fell upon Pompeii, went up Vesuvius twenty-two times and bought the Portland Vase for 1,000 guineas. Emma voyaged out to Naples with mother, under the impression that she was visiting him to better her education in music and dancing. In 1786 she became his mistress, despite having written to Charles Greville in Paddington: 'If I was with you I would murder you and myself both . . . I never will be his mistress.'

Five years later, Sir William became a Privy Counsellor and married Emma in London. She was literally an entertaining hostess, playing the harpsichord, singing loudly and striking attitudes – depicting emotions by *tableaux vivants* in drapes, just like being a Goddess of Health. She had 'the ease of a barmaid not of good breeding', murmured an English visitor. Sir William thought she was wonderful, and led the clapping.

Emma had made a fuss of Nelson when they had already met in September 1793. He had landed in Naples with dispatches from Admiral Hood, who had just taken Toulon, Versuvius erupting in befitting splendour above. His second visit was more dramatic – the midnight escape of King, Queen, courtiers, nobles and the

Hamiltons in small boats under the noses of the treacherous Neapolitan Jacobins, with dark lanterns, whispered orders, cocked pistols, drawn cutlasses, all aboard the *Vanguard*, sailing at dawn for Palermo – then everyone seasick during a day's delay from the violent storms. The refugees arrived in Sicily after Christmas, Sir William Hamilton went to bed with an attack of the bile, and Emma and Nelson became infatuated with each other, he through admiration of her stiff upper lip, she through his admirable efficiency as their saviour. Diplomatic social life resumed in Palermo, Sir William stayed in bed, Emma and Nelson took to it.

Nelson was back in Naples on 24 June, representing King Ferdinand. He forced the insurgents' surrender and caught its leader, Admiral Prince Caracciolo, who was escaping disguised as a peasant. Nelson court-martialled him aboard the flagship *Foudroyant*, and two hours after the verdict he was dining on board with the Hamiltons when a signal-gun announced his prisoner hanged from the yard-arm of a Neapolitan frigate, then thrown overboard. Such vindictive effort was marred by the Admiral's reappearance – bloated, discoloured, eyes starting in strangulation from their sockets – floating upright, ballasted by his manacles, bobbing under King Ferdinand's eyes aboard *Foudroyant* one early morning shortly afterwards.

Nelson was ordered to Minorca, but he invoked Admiralty outrage by refusing to obey (he said he was busy with the siege of Malta), and instead passed a year in Naples living with the Hamiltons. It was *la dolce vita* (though Emma was putting on weight). Nelson was on £2,000 a year pension from an appreciative Parliament and £10,000 from the East India Company, and King Ferdinand had made him Duke of Bronte, in Sicily, at £3,000 a year, even though the money never arrived. Nelson henceforth signed his seaborne letters to Emma with his two titles 'Nelson & Bronte', inciting the wild speculation upon opening their volume that he was created by the authoress of *Wuthering Heights*.

Emma had the precious ability of making life seem fun, which was so uplifting for Nelson, whose life was passed among those making it the opposite. He was famous, but it was she who made him feel it the most delightfully. He was emotionally and socially gauche, and Emma made both irrelevant. Better still, Sir William was pushing seventy and went to bed after supper, leaving him to entertain Emma for the rest of the night. In February 1799, he wrote to Emma that she had taken 'those liberties with me which no woman in this world but yourself ever did', and on 12 February 1800 Nelson logged that they had copulated.

It was all so civilised, in the spirit of British Empire building; the natives called them the *tria juncta in uno*. Emma's intimacy with Maria Carolina was strengthened by the Queen's hatred of the French after they had guillotined her sister in 1793. Nelson pressed upon the Admiralty Emma's 'eminent services' in this privileged position in gathering intelligence and procuring supplies, but the Admiralty disbelieved him.

That November, Nelson went home on sick leave. The Hamiltons came too. After a journey mostly overland (their signatures are displayed in a visitors' book in Prague) the three landed in a storm at Yarmouth. On 30 January, Emma had a daughter at 23 Piccadilly, whom she called Horatia. 'Our loved Horatia,' Nelson wrote fervently to 'my own dear Wife, in my eyes and the face of Heaven'. Sir William the diplomat accepted his own child without quiver of eyebrow.

Meanwhile, what of Fanny?

On the first Christmas of their marriage, they went to live for five years at Burnham Thorpe rectory in Norfolk, Nelson's family home. Afterwards, they lodged in Bath, and in 1797 Nelson bought Roundwood for £2,000, a four-bedroomed house standing in fifty acres near Ipswich. Fanny got the place nice for a sailor home from the sea, but she was not much of a housewife without the slaves. She muddled the laundry and infuriated Nelson by sending him to sea with skimpy kit. She wrote to him conscientiously, telling him about the weather at home and how the garden was coming along and sending him jars of cherries in brandy and pots of apricot jam. But when the national hero returned after three years, arriving at Roundwood from Yarmouth with a cavalry escort, Fanny was not at home. She had muddled things again, and was waiting for him in London.

They met at a hotel in St James's. Dinner – the Hamiltons joined them – was difficult. Nelson and Fanny lived together in Mayfair, while Nelson began to worry that the future Prince Regent had his lusty eye on Emma. One morning in December, Fanny stood up at breakfast and announced: 'I am sick of hearing of dear Lady Hamilton and am resolved that you shall give up either her or me!' Nelson walked out and rejoined the Fleet.

A year later, Fanny wrote to him from a rented house in Marylebone:

> ... which I have now to offer for your
> accommodation is a comfortable, warm house. Do,
> my dear husband, let us live together. I can never
> be happy until such an event takes place. I assure
> you again I have but one wish in the world, to
> please you. Let everything be buried in oblivion,
> it will pass away like a dream. I can now only
> entreat you to believe that I am most sincerely
> and affectionately your wife, Frances M. Nelson.

To which Nelson responded:

> Opened by mistake by Lord Nelson, but not read.

But he settled on her £1,200 a year.

Nelson was then living at Merton Place in Surrey, with the River Wandle, which enters the Thames at Wandsworth, flowing past the end of the garden. Emma had found it in 1801 and Nelson had bought it for £9,000. Merton, not Roundwood, was Nelson's romantic home, of which he wrote longingly to Emma at sea (though when he mentioned the 'thatched cottage' he was being anatomical, not architectural). With them lived Sir William, and the Hamiltons' visiting friends. Wrote their guest Lord Minto about Emma:

> ... she and Sir William and the whole set of them are living with him at his expense. She is in high looks, but more immense than ever. She goes on cramming Nelson with trowelfuls of flattery, which he goes on taking as quietly as a child does pap.

The London papers were beginning to run heavy jokes – like Emma remarking in the smoking-room that Nelson's pipe drew more vigorously than her husband's. Sir William started to feel irritation in his smooth diplomatist's skin. The couple began to squabble. He wrote to Emma pathetically:

> I am arrived at an old age when some repose is really necessary and I promised myself a quiet home and altho' I was sensible, and said so when I married, that I should be superannuated when my wife should be in her full beauty and vigour of youth, I by no means wish to live in solitary retreat, but to have seldom less than twelve to fourteen at table, and those varying continually, is coming back to what was so irksome to me in Italy ... I have no complaint to make, but I feel that the whole attention of my wife is given to Lord N, and his interest in Merton. I well know the

purity of Lord N.'s friendship for Emma and me, and I know how very uncomfortable it would make his Lordship, our best friend, if a separation should take place . . . As I cannot expect to live many years, every moment to me is precious, and I hope I may be allowed sometimes to be my own master and pass my time according to my own inclination . . .

On 6 April 1803 he died, in the arms of Emma and Nelson.

A month later, the pair christened their two-year-old, who was living with her nurse in London, as Horatia Thompson, Lord Nelson's god-daughter, no parentage offered. They had another child in the early days of 1804, who was dead by March. Before he sailed from Portsmouth aboard *Victory* on 15 September 1805, their relationship was blessed at communion. They exchanged wedding rings and Nelson assured Emma before the clergyman: 'Our friendship is most pure and innocent and of this I call God to witness.'

The man who rises 167 feet 6½ inches above Trafalgar Square deserves another modest monument to his mastery of the *ménage à trois*.

As Lord Minto further observed, the last time he saw Nelson before his sailing for Trafalgar: 'He is in many points a great man, in others a baby.'

After Trafalgar, Emma so often fainted in public when the tenor John Braham sang his hit 'The Death of Nelson' that she was suspected of going to the theatre for that purpose.

The death of Sir William Hamilton, and two and a half years later of Nelson, left Emma with £2,000 a year. By 1808 she owed £18,000, and in 1813 she was arrested for debt. With the connivance of a City alderman she escaped from King's Bench prison and fled to Calais. The spiteful said that she took to drink and lived in poverty;

but she could share Horatia's legacy, her letters recorded enjoying turbot, partridge and a good Bordeaux, and her funeral cost £28. 10s. She died five months before Waterloo, and, like its burghers, she has a statue in Calais.

In 1822, Horatia wed the vicar of Tenterden among the hop-fields of Kent, had eight children and died in 1881.

In 1893, Sir William Fraser Bt, a gossipy former MP, discovered a story about fourteen-year-old Napoleon at his Military Academy in Champagne.

> We cannot picture to ourselves the first Emperor of the French hitching up his loose trousers, and requesting in English his brother sailors to 'Belay' nor 'Avast heaving!' We cannot fancy him requesting anyone to 'Shiver his timbers', nor indeed to use any of the naval vernacular; such at least as it is represented on the British Stage.
>
> Yet this state of things was not far from occurring. When Napoleon was at school at Brienne, the son of an English Peer, who himself became Lord Wenlock, was his schoolfellow. One day the little Corsican came to young Lawley, and said 'Look at this'; he showed him a letter written in remarkably good English: it was addressed to the British Admiralty; and requested permission to enter our Navy. The young Buonaparte said 'The difficulty I am afraid will be my religion.' Lawley said 'You young rascal; I don't believe that you have any religion at all.' Napoleon replied 'But my family have: my mother's race, the Ramolini, are very rigid: I should be disinherited if I showed any signs of becoming a heretic.' These facts I had from one who had very good means of knowing: he told me that Buonaparte's letter was sent: and that it still exists in the archives of the Admiralty. I have not searched for it; for the simple reason that I did not wish so good a story to become prematurely public. I hope that someone who has access to the

historical documents in that department may take the trouble to find it.

Nobody did take the trouble. Napoleon could have been our Nelson. But whom would he have so gloriously fought?

SIX

A Sound of Revelry by Night

· ·

Meanwhile Wellington continued to arouse the unbounded
enthusiasm of women. As was his way, he made no bones
about it when people questioned him. After the great days
in Paris were over a lady asked him if it was true that he
had received all that female adulation.
    'Oh yes! Plenty of that! Plenty of that!' replied the Duke
breezily.

> Elizabeth Longford, *Wellington: the Years of the Sword*

· ·

The Iron Duke

On 12 September 1805, a major-general ten years younger
than Nelson was waiting in Downing Street to see Lord
Castlereagh, the Secretary of State for War and the Colonies, when he was joined in the ante-room by:

> ... a gentleman, whom from his likeness to his
> pictures and the loss of an arm, I immediately
> recognised as Lord Nelson. He could not know who
> I was, but he entered at once into conversation
> with me, if I can call it conversation, for it was
> almost all on his side and all about himself and,
> in reality, in a style so vain and so silly as to surprise
> and almost disgust me.
>   I suppose something that I happened to say may
> have made him guess that I was *some-body* and
> he went out of the room for a moment, I have no

doubt to ask the office-keeper who I was, for when he came back he was altogether a different man, both in manner and matter. All that I had thought a charlatan style had vanished and he talked of the state of the country and of the aspect and probabilities of affairs on the Continent with a good sense and a knowledge of subjects both at home and abroad that surprised me equally and more agreeably than the first part of our interview had done; in fact, he talked like an officer and a statesman.

This was echoed in the autumn of 1870 at St George's Hall in London, when W. S. Gilbert first met Arthur Sullivan and, remembering an incomprehensible sentence in the *Encyclopaedia Britannica*, pulled his leg by suggesting:

> I maintain that if a composer has a musical theme to express, he can express it as perfectly upon the simple tetrachord of Mercury, in which (as I need not tell you) there are no diatonic intervals at all, as upon the much more complicated dis-diapason (with the four tetrachords and the redundant note) which embraces in its perfect consonance all the simple, double and inverted chords.

Sullivan asked helplessly for the question to be repeated, confessed that he would have to think it over, and decided not to do the music for Gilbert's latest operetta.

Wellington and Nelson never enjoyed the fruitful collaboration of Gilbert and Sullivan, for that day in Downing Street was the only one on which they met. 'Now, if the Secretary of State had been punctual and admitted Lord Nelson in the first quarter of an hour, I should have had the same impression of a light and trivial character that other people have had, but luckily I saw enough to be satisfied that he was really a very superior man,' Wellington decided, aiming accurately at the Nelson touch.

Ten years later, on a shooting party:

> The Duke of Wellington, slightly ragged on his return from Waterloo, hit a cow, a dog and an aged countrywoman. The Duke's hostess Lady Shelley told her: 'My good woman, this is the proudest moment of your life. You have been shot by the greatest Englishman alive.'

Wellington had succeeded Nelson in the Pantheon. His sexual expeditions were similarly curious.

Harriette Wilson's *Memoirs* of 1825 are jolly, lively and resonant with the ring of untruth.

> I was getting into debt, as well as my sister Amy, when it so came to pass, as I have since heard say that the – immortal!
> No; that's common; a very outlandish distinction, fitter for a lady in a balloon.
> The terrific! that will do better. I have seen his grace in his cotton nightcap. Well then; the terrific Duke of Wellington! the wonder of the world! ...

Harriette recalled that year when Nelson met Wellington, the major-general just home victoriously from India:

> ... who, feeling himself amorously given – it was in summer – one sultry evening, ordered his coachman to set him down at the White Horse Cellar in Piccadilly, whence he sallied forth on foot to No. 2 or 3 in Berkeley Street, and rapped hastily at the door, which was immediately opened by the tawdry, well-rouged housekeeper of Mrs Porter, who, with a significant nod of recognition, led him into her mistress's boudoir and then hurried away, simpering, to acquaint the good Mrs Porter with the arrival of one of her oldest customers.

84

Mrs Porter, on entering her boudoir, bowed low;
But she had bowed lower still to his grace, who
had paid but shabbily for the last *bonne fortune*
she had contrived to procure him.

'Is it not charming weather?' said Mrs Porter, by
way of managing business with something like
decency.

Wellington did not comment on the weather, but
claimed that a beautiful girl had just 'come out', a very
fine creature called Harriette. Mrs Porter assured him
that she had already fulfilled three applications that very
month for Harriette. 'My good woman,' said Wellington
with customary briskness, 'my time is precious. One
hundred guineas are yours, and as much Harriette's, if
you can induce her to give me the meeting.'

Harriette was nineteen, pert-faced and wild. 'The girl
must be mad!' exclaimed Lord Melbourne, Queen Victoria's first Prime Minister, when his own son was un-
successfully hunting her. 'She looks mad. I thought so
the other day, when I met her galloping about, with her
feathers blowing, and her thick dark hair about her ears.'

She was then fifteen, starting out as Lord Craven's
mistress on Royal Parade, Brighton. He kept drawing her
pictures of cocoa trees, but 'so miserably tired was I of
Craven, and his cocoa trees, and his sailing-boats, and
his ugly, cotton nightcap . . .'

Harriette had a thing about nightcaps. '"Surely," I
would say, "all men do not wear those shocking nightcaps; else all women's illusions had been destroyed on
the first night of their marriage!" I wonder, thought I,
what sort of a nightcap the Prince of Wales wears?'

So she wrote to the Prince: '. . . if you pity me, and
believe you could make me in love with you, write to
me, and direct to the post office here.' By return, an aide
invited: 'If Miss Wilson will come to town, she may have

an interview,' but nothing came of it, a regrettable loss to her of literary material.

Harriette was the daughter of a Swiss clockmaker with a shop in Mayfair, and she was now serving the aristocracy as estimably as Lock's the hatters in St James's. She received Wellington three afternoons later, punctually at three, at her home in Sommers Town on the north fringe of London, between Lord's Cricket Ground and the Smallpox Hospital. Wellington said, 'How do you do?' and reached for her hand.

> 'Really,' said I, withdrawing my hand, 'for such a renowned hero, you have very little to say for yourself.'
> 'Beautiful creature!' uttered Wellington.
> 'Good gracious!' said I, out of all patience at his stupidity, 'what come you here for, duke?'
> 'Beautiful eyes, yours!' explained Wellington.
> 'Aye, man! they are greater conquerors than ever Wellington shall be; but, to be serious, I understood you came here to try to make yourself agreeable?'
> 'What, child! do you think that I have nothing better to do than to make speeches to please ladies?' said Wellington.

He called constantly, addressing her with his stylish soldierly succinctness. He liked her because there was no humbug about her. She found her new client unentertaining, and in the evenings, 'when he wore his broad red ribbon, he looked very like a rat-catcher'.

In the early summer of 1808:

> The Duke of Wellington, who, I presume, had discovered the tough qualities of his heart, which contributed to obtain him such renown in the field of battle, possessed no more merit for home service or ladies' uses than did his good digestion,

betook himself again to the wars. He called to take a hasty leave of me a few hours before his departure.

'I am off to Spain directly,' said Wellington.

I know not how it was but I grew melancholy when I was about to say, 'God bless you, Wellington!' I burst into tears. They appeared to afford rather an unusual unction to his soul, and his astonishment seemed to me not quite unmixed with gratitude.

'If you change your home,' said Wellington, kissing my cheek, 'let me find your address at Thomas's Hotel, as soon as I come to England; and, if you want anything in the meantime, write to Spain; and do not cry; and take care of yourself: and do not cut me when I come back.'

'Do you hear?' said Wellington; first wiping away some of my tears with my handkerchief; and then, kissing my eyes, he said, 'God bless you!' and hurried away.

'I have thought of you very often in Spain,' he confessed on his return, 'particularly one night, I remember, I dreamed you came out on my staff.' There was a tenderness between them. Better still, he paid well. 'Wellington had relieved me of many duns, which else had given me vast uneasiness,' Harriette acknowledged gratefully.

The writing of Harriette's *Memoirs* was inspired by the meanness of her client the Duke of Beaufort, who substituted a down payment of £1,200 for a promised £500 annuity. Their publication in 1825 was by John Joseph Stockdale in four paperback parts, and the sale was so gratifying that crush barriers had to be erected at his shop in Opera Colonnade in the Haymarket, the crowds ten deep on the morning of each new volume's detonation. To their fury, many of the fashionable and noble, such as Lord Melbourne's son the Hon. Frederick Lamb, were unable to lay hands on a copy to see if they were in it.

Lamb threatened Harriette 'with prosecution, death and destruction, if his conduct towards me in time, auld lang syne, was printed'; she reflected sorrowfully that had he 'only opened his heart, or even purse, to have given me but a few hundreds, there would have been no book, to the infinite loss to all persons of good taste and genuine morality'. In St James's, White's and Brooks's clubs held emergency meetings and resolved never to buy the book, but of course everyone did to see what it said about their fellow members.

The only recorded plaintiff was Mr Blore, a Piccadilly stonemason. He had assured Harriette: 'You'll find me a very reasonable, good-natured fellow: and, as for going to the play, if you are fond of that, I can get orders for the pit, whenever I like.' Her comment on his proposal of marriage: 'It is morally and physically impossible for a woman, be she what or whom she may, to attach herself to anything so low and vulgar as this poor Mr Blore,' won him £300. He must have tested her more than the unlitigious Lord 'Fred' Beauclerc, 'a sly, shy, odd man, not very communicative, unless one talks about cricket'.

Harriette's book ran to a hand-rubbing thirty editions in a year, and the following one it appeared in French, with coloured plates.

The book's pointed references to Johnson and Molière and Voltaire, its liberal scattering of Shakespeare and earnest interviews with Byron, urge that Stockdale ghosted it. He was a liveryman of the Stationers' Company, a pushy publisher who twelve years later successfully took on the House of Commons. They printed a report that he had supplied obscene books to the prisoners in Newgate, and the courts rejected parliamentary privilege because publishing was not an essential function of Parliament. Unfortunately, when the sheriffs tried to extract Stockdale's libel damages, Parliament imprisoned them and won its case by changing the law.

The enterprising Stockwell had already established subsidiary rights in the *Memoirs* by inviting its characters to pay for their exclusion at £200 a go. A week before publication, he wrote to Wellington exclaiming that he had stopped the presses, because of 'various anecdotes of your Grace which it would be most desirable to withhold, at least such is my opinion'. Wellington wrote across the letter the nascent catchphrase 'Publish and be damned' and returned it: or perhaps he did not, no more than Disraeli truly defined 'lies, damned lies and statistics', or Mrs Thatcher discovered 'there is no alternative', or Mr Wilson learned that 'a week is a long time in politics'. Wellington anyway captures triumphantly the English language prize attrib.

Stockdale protested in return that 'his chief motive was to protect, as well as he could, any friend who might be disagreeably implicated in the book. Instead of exulting, he was grieved & pained, far, very far beyond what he shall attempt to describe, in the discovery of the prominent figure which the Duke of Wellington & the Marquess Wellesley cut, in those pages, from which S. was anxious to obliterate them.' He added that he owned half of the action, and cutting the Wellington copy would knock £5,000 off the sales figures. 'S. does not hesitate to say that twice that sum would be a cheap purchase of the destruction of those details, which a few hours will place beyond the possibility of redemption,' he ended, with a businesslike unctuousness from which the publishing trade has not wholly freed itself.

Sir Walter Scott thought 'the wit is poor', but wrote of the *Memoirs* in his *Journal* at the end of 1825:

> ... there is some good retailing of conversations, in which the style of the speaker, so far as known to

me, is exactly imitated . . . Some one asked Lord
Alvanley, himself very sorrily handled from time
to time, if Harriette Wilson had been pretty correct
on the whole. 'Why, faith,' he replied, 'I believe
so . . .' I think I once supped in her company more
than twenty years since at Mat Lewis's, where the
company, as the Duke said to Lucio, chanced to be
'fairer than honest'. She was far from beautiful . . .
but a smart saucy girl with good eyes and dark hair,
and the manners of a wild schoolboy.

Perversely, the ring of untruth can be misheard, particularly when it makes good reading.

Harriette married a colonel, went to live in the rue du
Faubourg St Honoré, and died in 1846.

In 1805, Wellington had proposed by letter to Lord
Longford's daughter Kitty Packenham, whom he had previously proposed to in 1793. He married her in Dublin
in 1806, at the entry of the bride muttering to the clergyman – his brother – 'She has grown ugly, by Jove!' The
marriage was anaemic in love and sore with friction. 'No
woman ever loved me, never in my whole life,' he
decided later. He confessed that he married Kitty because
he did not think he would care for anyone else, and
anyway he would be away with the Army.

While Napoleon was kicking his spurs on Elba in the
summer of 1814, Wellington was ambassador to Paris. In
the jollity of conquest he reputedly commandeered two
of Napoleon's mistresses, the contralto Giuseppinna
Grassini and Mademoiselle George the actress. Mademoiselle George proclaimed that Wellington '*était de beau-
coup le plus fort*', but under the circumstances she
would, wouldn't she?

'The vulgar belief concerning the Duke that he was
profligate among women was utterly unfounded,'
declared Wellington's Chaplain-general of the Forces –
but he would, too, wouldn't he?

Wellington had paler girl-friends than Harriette Wilson. When Mrs Harriet Arbuthnot read of the other Harriette she was dumbstruck with disbelief, or perhaps envy. Mrs Arbuthnot was dark and good-looking, with big brown eyes, and had known Wellington from childhood, being twenty-five years younger than he was and twenty-seven years younger than her husband. An accusation of his wife being Wellington's mistress reached Mr Arbuthnot anonymously from Charles Greville, who managed the Duke of York's stud and wrote his own *Memoirs*, and whose mother's romance with Wellington had been extinguished by his father. But his letter – his writing was spotted – caused only earnest matrimonial discussion and a resolution to be more wary in future. Lady Shelley, who apologised for Wellington shooting the peasants, and herself a hero-worshipper who nearly fainted when she first spoke to him, wrote bitchily that Wellington admired Mrs Arbuthnot so greatly because 'she had a manlike sense – but Mrs Arbuthnot was devoid of womanly passions, and was, above all, a loyal and truthful woman'.

Wellington's wife died in 1831. Mrs Arbuthnot died on 1 August 1834 aged forty-one, five days after a pleasant lithograph appeared of the pair strolling arm in arm in Hyde Park, with her looking tenderly at what Byron called his 'eagle beak, the hook whereon he suspends the world'.

Then began the weird correspondence of seventeen years between Wellington and Miss J.

Miss Anna Marie Jenkins of 42 Charlotte Street, Portland Place, London, enjoyed a religious enthusiasm which she let loose into fanaticism. Wellington's letters – always addressed to 'Miss J' – and her diaries were found in the 1880s in a trunk in the attic of a country house 'within thirty miles of New York city'. Wellington's jerky, increasingly crabbed handwriting was unchallengeable; so was his style.

Early in 1834, she had just extracted confession, repentance and conversion from a condemned murderer, outdoing the persuasion of both the Catholic and Protestant clergy. She felt that God now called her to greater work. Looking round for an object, she descended upon the Chancellor of Oxford University the Duke of Wellington, though ignorant of the date of the Battle of Waterloo and the name of the victor. Miss J wrote to Wellington about the necessity of his rebirth into righteousness and left a Bible with the porter at his home, Apsley House, 'No. 1, London', at Hyde Park Corner, with an invitation to visit her.

'Although the Duke is not in the habit of visiting young unmarried ladies with whom he is not acquainted,' he replied, 'he will not decline to attend Miss J.' In November, he appeared. She was twenty, and gorgeous. 'Oh, *how* I *love* you! *how* I *love* you!' he exclaimed at once, much as he had enthusiastically introduced himself to Harriette Wilson. She responded by saying: 'I will show you *my Treasure!*' but it was only her Bible.

Sixty-five-year-old Wellington explained to his lovely saintly hostess that his feeling was inspired by God. She perceived that he intended marriage, but when he called again before Christmas a changed assessment of his designs brought doubt about the propriety of letting him through the door.

> I do not consider it right personally to place myself
> so fully and confidentially in the power of one
> who, however honourable and noble, occasionally
> seems to forget he is confided in by a Being who
> *feels* herself entitled even in the sight of God, not

only to the appellation of virtuous, in the strictest
acceptation of the word – but RIGHTEOUS,

she wrote with anaphrodisiac prissiness.

Says her biographer of 1889, the American Presbyter-
ian minister's daughter Christine Herrick:

> Miss J was impulsive, enthusiastic and
> undisciplined. Whatever she did was done with all
> her might. In her sight there could be no middle
> course, no half-way measures. By much
> introspection and pondering of the Scriptures she
> developed into a religious zealot, frantically anxious
> for the conversion of those about her. And this
> conversion was in her mind nothing less than the
> turning aside from all worldly pursuits, and the
> entire dedication of time and self to religious
> avocations. She shrank with horror from what she
> called 'The World', and interpreted this to mean
> public offices, wealth, and honours conferred by the
> State. All these she considered as snares to draw
> the soul from the contemplation of God and
> eternity, and bind it down to the things of time
> and sense.

Why two so disparate beings should have troubled the
Post Office is puzzling. Miss J renounced 'The World';
Wellington was made by it and he shaped it – but fame
is the spur that energises letter-writing nutters. Miss J's
epistolary style combined the evangelical and the unin-
telligible; Wellington's was as practical as a cookery-
book. He confessed to her politely: 'The Duke is unfortunately for him not sufficiently informed to enable Him
to write upon some of the Higher and more sacred Top-
icks of Miss J's Letters.'

Her subjects varied from the adversities of stagecoach
travel – to which he replied on 3 August 1835:

MY DEAR MISS J., – ... There is always Inconvenience in travelling in a Stage Coach. It cannot be otherwise ... The Inconvenience felt in England is of a moral and mental description. It is formed of the trash and nonsense which a traveller is condemned to hear in these vehicles; because every body talks; and says not what he thinks but what the fancy of the Moment suggests. For this which was the particular Inconvenience which you suffered upon this Journey, there is no remedy, but *Patience*; and I would add *Silence*.

– to becoming the Duchess of Wellington. 'God influenced the Duke of Wellington to love me above every other lady upon earth from the first moment he beheld me,' she kept in mind, upon which he commented: 'What would be said, if I, a man of seventy years of age, nearly, were to take in marriage a lady young enough to be my Granddaughter?'

Miss J exclaimed to her diary:

Alas! Alas! how deceitful is the human heart! For I am convinced that although the Duke *wrote* thus, there was not a moment during our acquaintance when if I had *not* been by the *Grace of God* what I was and am that he would have thought I was too young to bow down before me with the most sinful adulation ... That I loved the Duke I am not ashamed to say, God knows, and that too with the purest affection. Consequently when he asked me if I felt sufficient to be with him a whole life (which was the question referred to in that odious letter, for odious indeed it still appears in my sight, yea, increasingly so with time, for I recoil with unspeakable horror from the thought that I could be thus enquired of without being clearly comprehended), I replied to the same in the following words, '*If it be the will of God*' ...

He responded: 'I received your Note. We perfectly understand each other; and with your permission I will call upon you tomorrow at three o'clock.'

Wellington rose at seven, went riding or striding out of doors, breakfasted at nine, never lunched, dined at seven – if pressed with work, alone, on a small round oak table in the library, letters around him as thick as autumn leaves. He answered all himself, on gilt-edged paper, polite to the courteous, rude to the irrelevant in the hope of spiking their pens. How he found time for Miss J is praiseworthy and baffling. He moved in high society, she in no society at all. But both were lonelyhearts. They were hard individuals, with difficulty in attracting or exuding soft emotions. Intimacy with another human is golden, even if struck by a freakish accident.

After 1836, they did not meet for eight years. She sent him hymns, parcels of tracts, 'Spectacle Wipers' (returned), 'Pen wipers' (kept), and offered a pointedly presbyopic 'Bible in large Print. That which I now have answers perfectly, and I will not deprive you of another.' In November 1849, she sent letters to the previous Prime Minister:

> I have received your letter of the 17th inst in which you have enclosed certain letters which you have written to Sir Robert Peel which I return! I am not the Post Man! nor the Secretary of Sir Robert Peel nor your Secretary! . . . To read one letter from you is as much as I can do.

And possibly a lock of her hair: 'The Duke of Wellington presents his Compliments to Miss J. She is quite mistaken. He has no Lock of Hair of Her's. He never had one . . .'

When she complained that he never signed his letters

95

with his name and closed them with a blank seal, he apologised:

> I always understood that the important parts of a
> Letter were its Contents. I never much considered
> the Signature; provided I knew the handwriting; or
> the seal, provided it effectually closed the letter . . .
> and the Seal frequently becomes heated, it is
> necessary to change it; and by accident I may have
> sealed a letter to you with a blank Seal.

When she offered to return all his letters, or to burn them, he advised: 'If you think proper, to send them in a parcel to my House: I will save you the trouble of committing them to the Flames.'

Wise fellow: a *billet doux* in the hand is worth an innumerable quantity still in the desk. Those which he himself had written to Lady Georgiana Fane were construed by her solicitors as grounds for breach of promise.

On 9 November 1850 Miss J wrote:

> O My dear Duke, for I cannot use formality under
> my present excited, distressed feelings, having
> been so shocked by that dreadful Advertisement in
> the Times of this day, saying you were gone forever!
> [A reported fatal fall while hunting in Lincolnshire,
> a hoax.] This God in His infinite mercy has proved
> to be false, having spared you, I trust for a far more
> glorious end than the one therein described. For
> this I can never thank him sufficiently, subscribing
> myself consequently with additional gratitude
> 'His devoted Child and Servant A. J.'

He replied on 21 December:

> Field Marshal the Duke of Wellington presents His
> Compliments to Miss J! He understood from a
> former letter; that it was Miss J's desire never to
> hear from the Duke again!

Therefore he did not write! nor should he write now! excepting a mere matter of Courtesy! He thus finally takes His leave!
WELLINGTON.

Miss J died in New York in 1862. Her list showed seventy-eight letters from Wellington in 1835, fifty-six in 1836, fifty-five in 1844, only three in 1848; 390 altogether. History caught up with *The Times* on 14 September 1852, when Wellington, Warden of the Cinque Ports, died in his armchair at Walmer Castle by the White Cliffs, aged eighty-three. The rusting Iron Duke was deaf, dyspeptic and lonely, with nobody to look after him but the servants and the local doctor, though the Earl of Stanhope called, and wrote *Conversations with Wellington*.

He became popularly the Iron Duke only late in life. Tennyson's 'Death of the Duke of Wellington' recalled Britain's 'ever-loyal iron leader's fame'. The Huguenot journalist Albany Fonblanque had mentioned 'the "iron Duke", the "hero of a hundred fights" ' in 1850.

The year before his death, Wellington had been an enthusiastic visitor to the Great Exhibition at Hyde Park, sheltered in the Crystal Palace – which he had freed of the bird-droppings which so agitated Queen Victoria with: 'Try sparrow-hawks, ma'am.' *Punch* was proud of conceiving 'The Crystal Palace' – though Andrew Marvell's 'Upon the Death of Lord Hastings' in 1649 begins a line: 'Before the crystal palace where he dwells . . .' It was from the iron shutters installed after 1831 on Apsley House, when Wellington's opposition to the Reform Bill incited Londoners to smash the windows, that *Punch* originally called him 'The Iron Duke'. Give a faithful dog a good name, and it sticks.

The Other Napoleon

Napoleon I was predominantly a success until he met his Waterloo; Napoleon III was predominantly a failure before he met his Chislehurst.

Napoleone Buonaparte of Ajaccio, as the first Emperor was called until he turned twenty-seven, had four brothers. Louis, nine years younger, became King of Holland as his stooge. Louis's third son became Napoleon III. Louis had married Hortense, the daughter of General Vicomte de Beauharnais, who was guillotined in 1794. Hortense's mother was Joséphine, who as the Viscomte's widow married Napoleon I. So the Emperor was Napoleon III's uncle and the Empress Joséphine was his grandmother.

The young Napoleon was seven at Waterloo, and banished to Switzerland. His elder brother having died of measles, the death of his cousin the King of Rome in 1832 created him head of the dynasty. His enthusiasm for ousting the restored Bourbon monarchy landed him first in New York, from where he returned to Switzerland on a false passport, and next, after his invasion of Boulogne by paddle-steamer in 1840, for the rest of his life in Ham Castle on the Somme, from where he escaped after five years to England.

Two years later, forty-one-year-old Napoleon ousted King Louis-Philippe and became President of the Second Republic; three years after that, he achieved a *coup d'état*, restored the Imperial title and sported the imperial beard. He ran the Second Empire in the name of the people (which generally means in the name of a few unpleasant people). He broke political parties, bloodily repressed protesters and stifled the press; but he buttered up the clergy as 'the restorer of overthrown altars', lavished the peasantry with cheap bread and holidays and he was good for business.

On 29 January 1853, Napoleon III married in Notre Dame Eugénie de Montijo, who was twenty-six, beautiful, frivolous and capricious, an ardent Catholic, a Spanish countess from Grenada (he had failed in a trawl of the daughters of the crowned heads of Europe). He doted on her and she much influenced him.

After a disastrous war against Prussia, Napoleon III found himself allegedly 'responsible for the ruin, invasion and dismemberment of France', and went to live with Eugénie in Chislehurst, now a south London suburb. He chose a country house which he had enjoyed in earlier exile, when he was after his host's sixteen-year-old daughter and swaddled her in Joséphine's furs. He died there after an operation for stone in the bladder by Queen Victoria's surgeon in January 1873, and was buried with appropriate ornament down the road in the village Catholic church – severely overloading it – until dug up and moved by rail to more commodious surroundings at Farnborough in Hampshire.

The Emperor lives on. His palace between bosky Chislehurst Common and the cricket pitch, spattered inside with the Imperial bee, is the fashionable golf club; the pub is the Imperial Arms, and when phone numbers were still beautified with adjectives the local exchange was IMPerial. A granite monument in the woods commemorates his son the Prince Imperial, killed in Zululand through the incompetence of the British, who always backed the Emperor: but as A. J. P. Taylor indicated, 'Napoleon III did no better with the British alliance than his uncle had done without it – unless it is better to die in Chislehurst than at St Helena.'

The Chislehurst connection is fitting because, in a further genealogical twist, Queen Victoria's Foreign Secretary might have been the Emperor's father-in-law.

In the autumn of 1832, the thirty-two-year-old British diplomat George Villiers, who was slim, fair, with a shapely mouth and downy sidewhiskers, was idling in Paris after negotiating a commercial treaty. He was to become Britain's most beautiful Foreign Secretary, outshining Sir Austen Chamberlain with his monocle and Sir Anthony Eden with his Clark Gable moustache and eponymous hat. He was noticed to be 'more *actively* kind than a hundred parsons put together'.

George Villiers encountered in Paris an old acquaintance, Madame de Montijo, whose husband was suffering temporary political banishment from Spain. 'She was beautiful, intelligent and gay, and in her apartment gathered at that time all that was smart and amusing in the social, political and artistic worlds,' recounted Villiers's grandson a century later. He added that Count Montijo was 'never on the best of terms with his wife' and that she was 'completely unprincipled'. Also, that his grandfather's earlier relationship with her 'had ripened into something deeper'.

The loving pair met again in Paris in 1855, during the Crimean War. George was now the Earl of Clarendon, an early chain-smoker of the newfangled Spanish cigarettes, and thought Napoleon III 'an odd little fellow'. He congratulated Madame de Montijo upon her daughter's brilliant destiny. How well he remembered the fair-haired child in her mother's apartment, which he had visited so often as an aspiring diplomat! Now she was the Empress Eugénie and, more delightfully still, princely pregnant. Madame de Montijo mentioned:

> And did Milord know that when the marriage was already declared the Emperor came to her in great distress of mind with a letter in his hand from some busybody who stated, what do you think? – oh, no really, it was too good – it stated that Eugénie was *Milord's daughter*! 'And what did you say to him?' asked Clarendon. The old Spanish woman looked

at him with the utmost simplicity. *'Sire,'* I said, *'les dates ne correspondent pas.'*

Fair enough.

Lady Clarendon was not amused.

> Funny story to repeat to George himself [she noted icily in her diary]. I did not know that she was aware of the report which has been so prevalent that the Empress was George's daughter, and as it is by no means a flattering report on her character, it seems queer that she should talk about it thus to him.

The Empress Eugénie quit Chislehurst for Hampshire and died in 1920 – when Charles de Gaulle was a thirty-year-old captain.

SEVEN

Victorian Values

· ·

But her remarks can freeze as well as crystallise. There is a
tale of the unfortunate equerry who ventured during dinner
at Windsor to tell a funny story with a spice of scandal or
impropriety in it. 'We are not amused,' said the Queen when
he had finished.

> Caroline Holland, *The Notebooks of a Spinster Lady*,
> *Tuesday, 2 January 1900*

· ·

A Sanitary Approach

What were Victorian values? Why did the Victorians
have them?

Sir Edwin Chadwick is the unsung eminent Victorian.
He was born in 1800 and died in 1890, an interesting
span from before the Battle of Trafalgar to after the first
motor car. He was called to the Bar in 1830, became
Chief Commissioner for the Poor Law in 1833, a member
of the Sanitary Commission in 1839, and of the Board of
Health in 1848. In 1871 he drained Cawnpore. He was
broad-faced, bald, with long black hair plastered across
the top and a straggly grey beard. He was an extremely
difficult man.

At thirty, Chadwick was the protégé of Jeremy
Bentham, who was fifty-two years older than he, and
who had been impressed by his articles in the fashionably

intellectual magazines. Bentham was the Victorian eminent in utilitarianism. His philosophy declared that our actions should be judged morally correct according to their maximising the pleasure, or minimising the pain, of those they affected. (The idea was given chic again 130 years later by Freud, with his Pleasure Principle: 'The ego strives after pleasure and seeks to avoid unpleasure.') Utilitarian to the last, Bentham left his body for dissection, and may be encountered today skeletally, wearing his everyday clothes, in the museum of University College Hospital in London.

Edwin Chadwick spent his life pursuing practically, and fiercely, Bentham's admirable doctrine of achieving 'the greatest happiness of the greatest number' through 'the sanitary idea'.

In 1831 cholera fell murderously on Britain. It arrived like the Black Death of 1348 from the Far East via India and Moscow. The epidemic killed 7,000 in London alone, and all the government could pit against it was a day of national fasting and penance. Another 10,000 Londoners fell to the epidemic of 1847, then 7,000 in 1849 and 11,000 in 1854. The Black Death germ was carried to humans by the bite of the rat flea; the germ of cholera, expelled by the human gut, flourishes in drinking water. Nobody at the pestiferous time knew this, microbes not having been discovered over the intervening 500 years.

Sweet Thames, run softly, with death. London shat into it and drank it.

Chadwick the sanitary evangelist was led by the nose. London stank. The open sewers and cesspits encroached everywhere, the unpaved streets were slimy with rotting litter and running with waste water, the cattle markets and slaughterhouses exhaled pungently, while tomorrow's joints and chops came mooing and baaing messily through the streets. There were the reeking tripe shops

103

and the gasworks, and in the festering burial grounds – bodies crammed one atop the other, 3,000 corpses to the acre, joined by 200 more every year – the rate of interment stinkingly outstripped the rate of decay.

The labouring classes, living one family to one room, might have a coffin leaking fluid and maggots among them for a fortnight before they could raise enough money for the funeral. Stench is no respecter of persons. On the warm afternoon of 30 June 1858, passers-by in a corridor of the newly built House of Commons were alarmed by the sudden and confused emergence from a committee-room of several MPs, led by Mr Disraeli, 'a mass of papers in one hand and with his pocket handkerchief clutched in the other, and applied closely to his nose, with body half bent'. He was followed by Mr Gladstone, also paying 'particular attention to his nose', and by others 'attacked by a sudden fit of expectoration', the disorder of the papers left behind 'showing how imperatively they had received notice to quit'. Their propulsion was the stink of untreated sewage, massed outside the windows at low tide on the banks of the Thames.

Chadwick believed that these inhaled smells caused fatal diseases. Eliminate them with cleanliness, and the noxious miasmas which wafted the odours about no longer menaced man with death. Despite obstruction and antagonism from the muddled-up government of London, and the indifferent government of the country, he established some sanitary order with cleanliness and deodorants (Eau de Cologne was the favourite). The sanitation of Britain owes much to the railways. The magnificent brick-lined tunnels dug by Irish navvies, speeding the puffing expresses under the sheep-strewn hills, were reproduced underground to flush the nation's excreta into the nearest water. London had eighty-two miles of sewers, four to twelve feet across, round or egg-shaped, draining by gravity into the Thames. The raw sewage was borne by the ebb-tides twenty-five miles downstream from London Bridge, to end up under the noses of the residents of Tilbury and Gravesend.

Fifty-two years after the first London cholera epidemic, Dr Robert Koch from the Rhineland, a pioneer into the world of germs, which lies like a deadly web upon our own, went scouring the cesspits of Egypt and India as chief of the German Cholera Commission. He discovered down his microscope the cause of cholera in the *vibrio cholerae* – a comma-shaped microbe with a long tail, all the better to swim with (he got 100,000 marks from the Prussian State for his trouble). By killing the germ with cleanliness, Chadwick had partially effected the cure without knowing the cause. Similarly, the worthily observant Dr Edward Jenner of Gloucestershire, in 1796, from studying the cowpox sores disfiguring the wrists of milkmaids, created vaccination against smallpox more than a century before its causative virus was found.

The middle class was evolving with the century. They were the shopkeepers, the tradesmen, the professional men, who were richly complimented in 1831 by Lord Brougham: 'I mean the middle classes, the wealth and intelligence of the country, the glory of the British name.' They were earnestly socially mobile. According to John Stuart Mill a few years later: 'To get out of one rank of Society into the next above it is the great aim of English middle-class life.' The defecatory habits of the middle class were, like their eating habits, becoming more polite.

Pepys did it in the drawing-room, on 'a very fine close stool'. In Edinburgh, they did it in chamber-pots and chucked it from the upstairs windows every morning, crying 'Gardy-loo!' In 1530, Erasmus was complaining that both Englishmen and their dogs did it in the rushes strewn across the floor. In the Palace of St Germain, on

8 August 1606, the Dauphin was noticed doing it against his bedchamber wall.

In the generous outer walls of medieval castles and monasteries, stone-seated closets crowned vertical shafts which dropped to a removable barrel at ground level, or into a pit cleaned out occasionally by men paid three times the going rate, getting 6d. an hour. Some closets within buttresses or turrets had an open drop into the moat, like the closet convenient for banqueters in the Tower of London. By the second half of the eighteenth century, when Chippendale and Hepplewhite were designing washstands, the closet and the bedside commode were becoming elegant furnishings in oak and marble and brass: Captain Anthorpe's smart Edwardian portable chemical closet, which caused such trouble in Evelyn Waugh's *Men at Arms*, went by the Indian Empire name of his 'thunder-box'.

The flushing water-closet, like the aeroplane, was a conception of Leonardo da Vinci. Queen Anne had a water-closet at Windsor, and by 1840 Queen Victoria had one in her Royal Saloon on the Great Western Railway. The first patent was taken out in 1775, for the 'Cummings', created by a Bond Street watchmaker. Water in a U-shaped bend formed a block between the pan and the waste-pipe, like a modern one. The 'Bramah', with the crank-operated valve, remained fashionable throughout the century, though smelly.

The 'Closet of the Century' had a swift emptying cascade, followed by a self-cleansing trickle, and was quiet enough not to proclaim its use throughout the home. The 'Pedestal Vase' could clear in a flush ten apples. The public lavatories at the Crystal Palace for the Great Exhibition of 1851, installed by Mr George Jennings, attracted 827,280 visitors to spend a penny. When the Crystal Palace was re-erected at Sydenham they risked redundancy, but they continued in action to make £1,000 a year. Mr Jennings foresaw 'Halting Stations' throughout London:

> Fancy one of these complete, having a respectable
> attendant, who on pain of dismissal should be obliged
> to give each seat a rub over with a damp leather
> after use, the same attendant to hand a clean
> towel, comb and brush to those who may require
> to use them. A shoe black might do a shining
> trade, as many go with Dirty Boots rather than stand
> exposed to the public gaze.

Such is civilisation.

As London oozed along the new railway lines to blot out the fields and villages with suburbs, its population grew from three-quarters of a million to three and a quarter million during Chadwick's lifetime. His problems were compounded by the demand for fresh water, and for sewage disposal, steadily increasing because of these fashionable water closets. He had impotently to smell his sewers turning into elongated stagnant cesspools.

The brotherhood of the Worshipful Company of Plumbers – its Letters Patent granted by James I, its Book of Ordinances established under Edward III in 1365, its arms blazoned with plumb lines and soldering irons – were busy laying the drains of countless new little homes all over the country, at 6s. 4d. a day on a sixty-hour week. The Prince of Wales, recovering from typhoid at Sandringham, declared that if he could not be a prince he would be a plumber.

With cheaply manufactured metal piping, plumbers veiled middle-class excretion with gentility (though users had to wait ten minutes between flushes, to fill up). Sound drains encourage respectability – so cherished, so feared to be lost into the insanitary squalor of the poor, in their stinking courts and human rookeries.

Respectability brought the nervous prudery that put pantaloons on piano-legs, called trousers unmentionables and reduced the wife to a husband's sanitary convenience. (Such aggressive gentility resurfaced a century later, when persons of small mind and vast self-importance uttered the absurd language of 'political correctness'.) The spiritual plumbers of the Church leapt to their opportunities and stopped the moral leaks. The Victorians' souls went to Heaven, and their bodies to graveyards of increasing salubriousness.

Drains were the foundation of the Victorian values – since glibly extolled but never defined.

Drains and drugs have brought more happiness to mankind that any political system or any politician. Communism or democracy cannot be measured against anaesthetics and antibiotics, no more than religion can be measured against frozen foods and patriotism against television: but the world would be pushed to choose which of these varied benefits to go without. The Victorians were blessed with anaesthetics at Christmas 1846; but another century had to pass before drugs could kill the germs which killed the mothers and infants, and medicine began to stretch the human lifeline.

Victorian values scorned divorce, but death regularly broke up marriages. The average duration of marriage at the start of Victoria's reign was nineteen years, so couples did not live long enough to get fed up with one another. In 1870, the British death rate was twenty-two per thousand, double today's. Only 7.5 per cent of the population made the age of sixty, compared with 21 per cent today. The retired couples who now make merry made only gravestones.

The Victorians did not much practise contraception. But with an infant mortality rate of over 150 per thousand live births, compared with 6.6 today, with childhood imperilled by many deadly fevers, a baby was welcomed into the family with tempered enthusiasm because it was unlikely to last. Half the deaths in London were of children under five. The Victorian expectation of life was forty for males and forty-three for females, and large families were born right up to the menopause, so the old couple would enjoy only a year or two's peace together after all their children had left home.

'The more things a man is ashamed of, the more respectable he is,' Bernard Shaw observed at the end of the Victorian age. The middle-class husband, master of his sound drains and his morals, had ready opportunity to enhance his respectability thus by enjoying sexual shame among prostitutes. The joy of marriage, and the angelical properties of women, were promoted to him regularly from the novel and the pulpit before he experienced either. He could shrug his shoulders at disappointment with the reality of both.

Their enumeration of prostitutes is as unreliable as that of flighting starlings, but the *Lancet* of 1857 awarded London 6,000 brothels and 80,000 tarts. The *Edinburgh Medical Journal* two years later gave up counting, adding that the evening stroller in certain streets of London, Glasgow or Edinburgh need not bother himself with statistics when 'his eyes and ears will tell him at once what a multitudinous amazonian army the devil keeps in constant field service, for advancing his own ends. The stones seem alive with lust, and the very atmosphere is tainted.'

Prostitutes swarmed along Haymarket, paraded between the snooty shops of the Burlington Arcade and decorated the music-hall bars and promenades. When the purity campaigners in 1894 got the Empire Theatre in Leicester Square to close its promenade, the canvas barriers were torn down by a youthful gang led by Winston Churchill. The Metropolitan police were at the time totting up 2,828 brothels and 8,600 prostitutes, but their exactitude was conservative. They overlooked the widespread casual sexual labour noticed by Thomas Hardy:

The Ruined Maid

'O 'Melia, my dear, this does everything crown!
Who could have supposed I should meet you in Town?
And whence such fair garments, such prosperi-ty?' –
'O didn't you know I'd been ruined?' said she.

– 'You left us in tatters, without shoes or socks,
Tired of digging potatoes, and spudding up docks;
And now you've gay bracelets and bright feathers
      three!' –
'Yes: that's how we dress when we're ruined,' said she.

– 'At home in the barton you said "thee" and "thou",
And "thik oon", and "theäs oon", and "t'other"; but
      now
You talking quite fits 'ee for high compa-ny!' –
'Some polish is gained with one's ruin,' said she.

– 'Your hands were like paws then, your face blue and
      bleak
But now I'm bewitched by your delicate cheek,
And your little gloves fit as on any la-dy!'
'We never do work when we're ruined,' said she.

– 'You used to call home-life a hag-ridden dream,
And you'd sigh and you'd sock; but at present you seem
To know not of megrims or melancho-ly!'
'True. One's pretty lively when ruined,' said she.

– 'I wish I had feathers, a fine sweeping gown,
And a delicate face, and could strut about Town!' –
'My dear – a raw country girl, such as you be,
Cannot quite expect that. You ain't ruined,' said she.

The Victorians put a practical value on their morals as on their drainage.

Queen Victoria

Queen Victoria was a passionate woman. She was (to her annoyance) less than five feet tall, plump, a hearty eater, partial to claret and whisky (she mixed them together in her glass at dinner), a hypochondriac obsessed with her bowels, short-tempered, vivacious, soft-hearted but stubborn, humorous and spasmodically giggly, emotional and sporadically hysterical. She married aged twenty Prince Albert, and in the twenty-one years until his death in 1861 had nine children spread over seventeen of them, the first born ten months and eleven days after her wedding.

Albert was tall, pale, fair, blue-eyed, with delicate moustache and whiskers. When he appeared at Windsor five months before the marriage she wrote in her diary, 'It was with some emotion that I beheld Albert – who is *beautiful*', despite his having been violently seasick all the way to Dover. He was a softie, an appreciative lover, a man of simple jokes and simple thoughts, a worthy propagator of both science and the arts, and an enthusiastic Prussian. He sighed resentment that he was (at £30,000 a year) the Queen's husband and not the master of her house, nor of her country, though he did a great job on the 1851 Exhibition and Wellington's funeral. Albert died aged forty-two from typhoid at Windsor, an ironic recompense for having replaced with water-closets the Hanoverian commodes and cleared its fifty-three overbrimming cesspits. Victoria agonisedly kissed his dead lips, spared infection by typhoid from such intimacy by her own immunising attack of the disease when aged sixteen.

Prince Albert in the Queen's emotional life was followed by John Brown, her Highland ghillie. He was burly and bushy-bearded, at Albert's death aged thirty-five, his face as stolid as Scots granite. He was always ornate in kilt, sporran and ribboned bonnet at her horse's head, even in Cannes. He was a devotee of the wee dram. The Queen transferred him from the chill mists of Balmoral to the sea breezes of Osborne on the Isle of Wight, promoting him to 'personal attendant' at £120 a year. She had developed a weakness for Highlanders, whom she found less vulgar and more intelligent than the English.

John Brown presented himself to Victoria every day after breakfast and lunch for his orders, cleaned her boots and her dogs, tucked her into her carriage-rugs, served her soup, spiked her tea with Scotch, hunted for marauding Fenians, addressed her with homespun Scots wisdom, and never took a holiday. She thought him an absolute treasure. He shortly became entrusted with bearing all the royal messages, including those to Prince Albert, when acting with the Queen's medium Robert James Lees during spiritualist sessions held in Windsor Castle. In 1866 he was believed to have married her (it was revealed by the *Lausanne Gazette* in Switzerland).

Victorian *Punch* developed a vulnerability for Scots jokes. Its cartoon figures in kilts and tweeds, with plaids and tam-o'-shanters and collies, conversed incomprehensibly in the captions (Mac precipitantly home from London: 'Mum, a had n' been the-erre abune two hours when – BANG – went saxpence!!!'). Picking on public grousing over the Queen's reclusive widowhood, *Punch* published in June 1866 an Imaginary Dispatch from Balmoral:

> Had the QUEEN been made aware that a
> Ministerial crisis was in the least likely to arise
> during the period which had been set apart for her
> visit to the Scotch, that visit would, of course,
> have been postponed until another season . . .
> The QUEEN is too well acquainted with the

sentiments of her subjects in reference to all her actions to suppose that they can ever be misinterpreted, but the Ministers who neglected to apprise her that they intended to take an early vote of Confidence ought to have seen that such neglect might justify the idea that the QUEEN, for the first time in her life, had allowed her own pleasure to interfere with the functions of Royalty.

The dig was followed by a sharper one, stealthily from the bottom of a column in July:

Court Circular, Balmoral, Tuesday

Mr JOHN BROWN walked on the Slopes. He subsequently partook of a haggis.

In the evening Mr JOHN BROWN was pleased to listen to a bag-pipe.

MR JOHN BROWN retired early.

Mr Punch's cudgel was snatched by the *John o'Groats Journal*, and Brown was assumed, in the impenetrability of Balmoral, to be the Queen's husband or lover. All Brown complained about was his feet swelling at night, from all the walking he had to do.

The Queen's ministers wanted to sack him. The Prince of Wales hated him. John Brown held the job for thirty-four years, until he died in 1883 at Windsor Castle from erysipelas, complicated by chronic alcoholism and delirium tremens.

Like many a middle-aged lady with time on her hands, the Queen felt she might have something to bestow upon the world through her pen. She had already published privately *Leaves* and *More Leaves from a Journal of Our Life in the Highlands*, which earned rave reviews from everyone who read it. She now settled at her desk to a biography of John Brown. The draft horrified her courtiers. Revelation of her sacred innermost feelings towards the man who cleaned her boots they suspected might be misinterpreted by normally salacious readers.

Also, it was dreadfully boring. But nobody dared tell her so. When the Dean of Windsor broke the critical silence, he was clobbered with outrage. Luckily, as with many books so earnestly begun, the author lost interest and it fluttered into the great wastepaper basket of literary eternity.

When John Brown died, the Queen wrote tearfully to the future George V that she had lost her irreplaceable 'dearest best friend'. To a courtier: 'the loss of the strong arm and wise advice, warm heart and cheery original way of saying things and the sympathy in any large and small circumstances is most cruelly missed'. To Brown's relatives: 'my grief is unbounded, dreadful, and I know not how to bear it'. In her last will, she specified that she hoped to meet him in Heaven.

When the Queen died in 1901, the inch and a half of charcoal filling the bottom of her coffin was decorated with a plaster cast of Prince Albert's hand and his dressing-gown. Then the Queen's other intimate adviser, her harassed doctor Sir James Reid, discharged his secret instructions. He approached her coffin alone, and installed into the corpse's left hand a case containing John Brown's photograph and a lock of his curly hair, which he hid with Queen Alexandra's flowers. He then packed the sides of the coffin with charcoal in muslin bags, they screwed down the lid, covered it with a white pall and passed it out to the waiting bluejackets.

Four years later, Reid handled the pay-off when Edward VII was blackmailed over a black trunk of three hundred letters, written by Queen Victoria to another doctor about John Brown, 'many of them most compromising'.

Whether she was Queen Chatterley or not is as impossible to tell as if King Alfred really burnt the cakes.

Mr Gladstone

Mr Gladstone was delightfully fond of Skittles. Skittles was the lovely brunette Catherine Walters, nicknamed also Anonyma, the *grande horizontale* of Victorian London, the Nell Gwynn of the 1860s. Like the Duke of Wellington's favourite courtesan, Harriette Wilson, fifty years before, Skittles was a dashing woman of racy speech and stylish clothes and elegant living. Sir Edwin Landseer painted her for the Royal Academy Exhibition of 1861, and the crowds blocked the gallery.

From five to seven every evening, nobody could drive from Wellington's Apsley House at Hyde Park Corner to Kensington Gore, because of the carriages following Skittles's outing in Hyde Park. 'Anonyma has fairly distanced her fair competitors,' went a letter to *The Times*, complaining about the traffic-jam. 'They can none of them sit, dress, drive, or look as well as she does; nor can any of them procure for money such ponies as Anonyma contrives to get – for love.'

Mr Gladstone ('Old Glad-eye' to the girls) became a close friend of this patently successful woman, always remembering her birthday and sending her lots of little presents. Skittles found him a much gayer man than the world credited, and he waltzed beautifully. 'In his grave manner he had an irresistible charm, and he was flattered by the company of beautiful women,' she gave a professional opinion. 'I do believe that secretly Gladstone had a mild passion for me. Never once did he give any hint of this except to say occasionally that our talks were something he would always cherish.'

Mr Gladstone's hobby was picking up and dusting down fallen women. This necessitated his roaming the streets of London after dark and engaging the ubiquitous prostitutes in conversation. He ventured only into the securer streets of Belgravia and Mayfair, on which walked the better sort of tart, and claimed a reclamation success-rate of twelve girls in three years (he had to settle one girl's long-standing stable bill, as she had given up work).

Nelly Fowler, whose very body-odour sent men mad, received Mr Gladstone at home, and found him a wonderful figure of a man, kind, considerate, polite, so handsome that she longed to stroke his magnificent head. Unexpectedly finding themselves talking to the Prime Minister on the Piccadilly pavement must have brought a gasp, even from girls to whom men were their stock-in-trade. How Mr Gladstone felt about it stayed unadmitted, though his eyebrow-raising friends suspected that it bettered the thrill of window-shopping for what you dared not buy.

Mr Gladstone may have ventured to the amatory shop-counter. He confessed to 'strange and humbling pursuits' with prostitutes, which was probably a whipping, popular among the gentry in the age of Swinburne. As a punishment for these lapses, Gladstone went home and flagellated himself. He stainlessly tried to close down brothels in Mayfair, though he encountered Parliamentary opposition over one in Pimlico, which conveniently served MPs.

Mr Gladstone in his seventies took a shine to Lillie Langtry, the actress and mistress of the Prince of Wales. She was passed to him for social betterment by the Prince (who was once castigated by Mr Gladstone for a 'squalid debauch' with a strange girl in Bonn). Mr Gladstone and the Jersey Lily dined often, and she sent letters coded to stay unopened by his secretaries – if rather too many of them for his tranquillity.

Mr Gladstone's sexual missionary work was shockingly unbelievable to Queen Victoria, until Mr Disraeli assured her warmly that it was all true.

Mr Disraeli

When Mr Gladstone, aged eighty-four, resigned for the final time as Victoria's Prime Minister on 2 March 1894, she responded shortly that: 'The Queen would gladly have conferred a peerage on Mr Gladstone, but she knows that he would not accept it.'

Mr Gladstone was mortified. So *that* was all she thought of him! He complained publicly that it reminded him of his once parting unceremoniously from the worthy mule which had plodded him all round Sicily.

The Queen had at first not much cared for his rival, dandyish Mr Disraeli, who was 'unprincipled, reckless and not respectable'. He kissed hands as her Prime Minister in 1868. Soon she was eating out of his.

> Disraeli was asked once why he did not propose
> such and such a measure to the Queen. 'Because,'
> he said, 'I must first be sure that it would have the
> approval of the two J.B.s' 'The two J.B.s?' 'Yes,' he
> explained, 'John Bull and John Brown,'

recorded *The Notebooks of a Spinster Lady* in 1879.

Mr Disraeli had a genius for realism.

Queen Victoria had already enjoyed a girlish pash on a Prime Minister. She was served at her accession by the twice-divorced Viscount Melbourne, who was aged fifty-eight, and his looks had gracefully faded since the days they had had to compete with Byron's. Melbourne fascinated and amused her. He educated her into her job, and he armed her with sophisticated values. He was so soppy about her, that whenever he talked of her to others he started to cry. Like John Brown, he was said by the chatterers to be marrying her.

Mr Disraeli had a way with him.

'We authors, Ma'am,' Mr Disraeli murmured to Queen Victoria, when her *Leaves from the Journal of Our Life in the Highlands* was the sure best-seller for 1868. 'Your Majesty is the head of the literary profession,' he assured her knowledgeably. Mr Disraeli sent her his novels, and she sent him primroses from the royal gardens, unconsciously founding the Tory Primrose League.

'The palace is not safe when the cottage is not happy,' was the sort of thing he warned her about. 'All great matters he would submit to her,' he promised, 'the burden of all trivial affairs should be borne by him alone,' while painstakingly doing the opposite. He called Victoria the Faery Queen. On 25 November 1875, he bought her the Suez Canal: 'It is just settled. You have it, Madam.' On 1 May 1876, he made her the Empress of India. What more could a woman want? 'I think he must have spread his butter very thick,' suggested one of the Queen's female friends.

Mr Disraeli became Lord Beaconsfield in 1876, having become a country gentleman in 1848 by buying Hughenden Manor in the Chilterns. He died in Curzon Street in 1881. When the Queen wanted to visit his deathbed, his famed reply, 'No, it is better not. She would only ask me to take a message to Albert,' displays realism to the last.

Mr Disraeli passed a realistic sex life. At twenty-one, he had a solicitor's wife, the ambitious bluestocking Sara Austin, whom he got (to keep it all secret) to copy the handwritten manuscript of his anonymous hit novel *Tremaine*. Seven years later, he was comfortably having Clara Bolton, wife of his Park Lane doctor, Buckley Bolton, a *mari complaisant*. A year later, it was Lady Henrietta Sykes, mother of four, though only after 12 August, Sir Francis Sykes being a keen grouse shooter.

All were women older than he was. When he married in 1839, it was an MP's widow, the chatty, flirty, rich Mrs Wyndham-Lewis of Park Lane, aged forty-six – twelve years older. He was badly in debt. 'Dizzy married me for my money, but if he had the chance again he could marry me for love,' she decided. Though she had to admit: 'He showed his affection and love to me while my first husband was alive.'

The Queen made her Viscountess Beaconsfield in her own right. At three in the morning, after a Commons triumph, over a tête-à-tête supper of Fortnum & Mason's pie and champagne, Mr Disraeli observed: 'Why, my dear, you are more like a mistress than a wife.' That was something to make a spouse think. Theirs was the marriage of true realistic minds.

Lord Palmerston

Prime Minister 1855–8 and 1859–65. When Foreign Secretary, in his fifties, he was nabbed bursting into one of the ladies-in-waiting's bedrooms at Windsor Castle. This augmented the Queen's hostility to Palmerston (his European policies contradicted the obviously correct ones of the European Prince Albert), which had reached the undiplomatic intensity of making her feel bilious if she read his speeches before dinner.

EIGHT

Victorian Vagaries

···

Forward, forward let us range,
Let the great world spin for ever down the ringing grooves
of change.
     Tennyson in 1842, under the misapprehension that trains
                      ran on tramlines

···

Exclusive to the Pall Mall Gazette

Red-headed and red-bearded William Stead was a crusad-
ing journalist. He was the son of a Congregationalist
minister, and in 1871, aged twenty-two, became editor
of the *Northern Echo* in grimy Darlington at £150 a year.
In 1878, the Salvation Army advanced upon and captured
Darlington. The Army was newly enlisted by General
William Booth, its war cry was 'Blood and Fire', its artillery was blaring brass bands, and within its uniformed
ranks marched sweeping-skirted tambourine-bashing
'Hallelujah Lassies', against whom the Darlington publi-
cans offered the feeble resistance of a £300 bribe to keep
quiet.

Stead took emotionally to the Salvation Army as
Kipling to the Empire.

This lively, locally famed journalist followed the familiar paper-chase to London. By 1883 he was editor of the
Pall Mall Gazette, which was modelled on Thackeray's

same fictitious title in being 'written by gentlemen for gentlemen'. Stead's predecessor was John Morley, who was to become a Cabinet minister, and who wrote four volumes on Gladstone and got a viscountcy. The *Gazette* was admirably informative and literary, but Stead made a more familiar success of it by transforming the paper into an organ of outraged sensationalism.

In 1885, Stead raised a conductor for lightning flashes of indignation about prostituted virginity. Virgins were the *bonnes bouches* on the sexual menu, at £25 a time. As the condition is pre-eminently temporary, the girls provided for customers were aged from about fifteen down to twelve – twelve being the age of consent, as it was the legal age of marriage. (Liverpool claimed to support five hundred prostitutes under thirteen, and there were specialist child brothels all over London, the best two run by Mrs Maxwell and Mrs Keeley in Whitechapel.) The children were mostly shipped from England to Brussels, which was the hub of the European virgin market, to be kept in notorious houses with the connivance of the Belgian *police des mœurs*, whose chief supplied the brothel-keepers' wine orders.

'Lovely creatures (for they do not care to take any who are not beautiful), innocent creatures who, stolen, kidnapped, betrayed, got from English country villages by artifice are sold to these human shambles,' wrote throbbingly Mrs Josephine Butler. Mrs Butler was a professional, if muddled, moral reformer. Her seventeen-year campaign to repeal the Contagious Diseases Acts – which she reasoned legally to sanction vice, through placing prostitutes under police supervision – achieved its triumph in Parliament in 1886, and immediately spread painful, disabling and deadly venereal diseases across the British Empire.

The brilliance of William Stead's heart-wringing prose could effortlessly transilluminate Mrs Butler's. He decided to apply it to the investigative journalism of buying a virgin, as later journalists pretended to buy drugs or official secrets to expose the wicked vendors. He readily won the backing of Mrs Butler, the Salvation Army, Cardinal Manning and the Archbishop of Canterbury. To play the part of a potential virgin rapist, he needed to defy a lifetime as a teetotaller and non-smoker and force himself upon champagne and cigars. His contact in the virgin business was Rebecca Jarrett, who had been a whore for twenty-four years – since she was twelve – but had seen the error of her ways and joined the Salvation Army. Though an MP mentioned to Stead that he could supply a hundred virgins at £25 apiece, if requested.

Rebecca Jarrett reckoned the wholesale price to be £4 down, and another £1 when the virginity had been professionally attested. On Derby Day 1883, she bought Eliza Armstrong, aged thirteen, from an unmarried couple in Marylebone. They went on a horse-bus to Madame Mourez in fashionable Dorset Square, a midwife who specialised in these cases, who certified her intactness. Then Rebecca took Eliza in a hansom to rooms over a ham and beef shop in Poland Street, Soho, an area where the commercialised rape of child virgins was to be overlooked.

Rebecca took Eliza's clothes off and tried to make her inhale chloroform, but Eliza disliked the smell. Stead appeared unexpectedly from the next room as her pretended seducer, and locked the door. Eliza screamed 'Take me home!' But she was taken to Harley Street, given more chloroform (professionally), examined by a surgeon who pronounced her still a virgin, was afforded a night's sleep in a hotel and in the morning taken to Charing Cross Station and put on the boat-train to Paris. The idea was to reproduce the routine export of virgins.

What a crammed day for a thirteen-year-old! More eventful than Alice's down the rabbit-hole.

At the beginning of July, the *Pall Mall Gazette* (usual circulation 12,000) trailed the story with a grave warning to 'all those who are squeamish, and all those who are prudish, and all those who prefer to live in a fools' paradise of imaginary innocence and purity, selfishly oblivious to the horrible realities which torment those whose lives are passed in the London Inferno', on no account to buy Monday morning's paper. Stead ran six pages of lurid sexual disclosure under the headline 'The Maiden Tribute of Modern Babylon', with 'The Violation of Virgins' and 'Strapping Girls Down' as subheadings to indicate the continuing shocking horrors. That evening, people were paying a shilling for a penny copy. Newsagents W. H. Smith did their bit for Stead by disgustedly refusing to handle it. The Salvation Army marched up and sold the copies instead; so did George Bernard Shaw as a matter of principle in the Strand.

The *St James's Gazette* complained about Stead: 'This shameless creature has flung all decency aside, openly dealing with the worst abominations in the plainest and foulest language.' The *St James's Gazette* was the rival paper. MPs pinched their noses in the Commons and vilified the gutter press, overlooking that the gutter provides the admirable service of handling the muck dropped into it. An MP demanded the author of such obscenities to be imprisoned, and the Home Secretary needed to reassure the House that there was nothing their countrymen were so determined to maintain as the purity of their homes. In the City of London, newsboys selling the *Gazette* were arrested.

For three days, Stead ran more stories of the virgin traffic. His readers continued resolutely to be disgusted and horrified. The *Gazette*'s offices by Trafalgar Square were besieged, and necessitated crush-barriers, like the publishers of Harriette Wilson's *Memoirs* in the Haymarket fifty-eight years earlier. As any layabout who got his hands on a few copies could sell them at a profit, there was an impatient riot and windows were smashed, and Stead complained furiously to the Home Secretary.

The series was syndicated in America, 100,000 bound copies were published in Paris, and the rights were sold across Europe. Stead had achieved an exemplary success of moral condemnation, at an exemplary profit. An unasked question was: whether the demand for child virgins represented an occasional deplorable idiosyncrasy, rather than the thriving lustful trade that he had so vividly denounced. Perhaps it was only a practical extension of the contemporary worship of little girls – by Lewis Carroll, John Ruskin, Samuel Rutherford Crockett of *The Lilac Sunbonnet*, and innumerable less articulate others.

Stead was only the outspoken messenger of depravity, but the Government wanted to prosecute him nevertheless. Then they had second thoughts: they would appear to be officially on the side of the rich virgin-violaters. The Salvation Army deafened Parliament with brass brands, escorting to Big Ben a petition two and a half miles long to raise the age of consent. In August, thirty-four Salvation Army brass bands gathered for a demonstration in Hyde Park, a prospect which rightly terrified the Government into raising the age to sixteen the week before.

After a hols in France, Eliza reappeared in Wimbledon, still a virgin. Rebecca Jarrett found herself charged with the child's abduction. Stead, on holiday in Grundewald, declaimed by telegraph: 'I alone am responsible . . . I am returning by the first express . . . to demand, if condemned, the sole punishment.' At the Old Bailey in October the judge obligingly gave him three months, disbelieving the Archbishop of Canterbury as his character witness.

Stead had defended himself at his trial, in his usual style. He did time in Coldbath Fields and Holloway, where he had an armchair, fire, desk, comfy bed and 'cosy little tea table'. They were, he declared, the happiest days of his life. Am I not the man of most importance now alive? he asked. He went back to the *Pall Mall Gazette*, then took up spiritualism, unpopularly supported the Boers in the South African war, and in 1912 achieved the ultimate in sensational moralistic journalism by going down with the *Titanic*.

DIY Enthusiasts

The Victorians suffered as many ludicrous sexual oddities as we do. They had a perverted horror of masturbation, which is as harmless as blowing your nose.

In 1857, Dr William Acton wrote *The Function and Disorders of the Reproductive Organs, in Childhood, Youth, Adult Age, and Advanced Life, Considered in their Physiological, Social and Moral Relations*.

Dr Acton was in his forties, a clergyman's son from Dorset, who learnt medicine at Bart's in London and in Paris under Philippe Ricord. Ricord was the famed venereologist from Baltimore, whom Oliver Wendell Holmes named 'the Voltaire of pelvic literature – a skeptic as to the morality of the race in general, who would have submitted Diana to treatment with his medical specifics, and ordered a course of blue pills for the vestal virgins'.

Acton qualified at the Royal College of Surgeons in 1840, and ran a prosperous venereal practice in fashionable Queen Anne Street. He discovered the appealing and profitable flair of writing popularly about his specialty. He published in 1870 *Prostitution, Considered in its Moral, Social, and Sanitary Aspects, in London and other Large Cities and Garrison Towns, with Proposal for the Control and Prevention of its Attendant Evils.* This directed minds to the medical control of prostitutes and inspired the Contagious Diseases Acts of 1886, which incurred the righteous, if mindless, fury of Mrs Josephine Butler. One of Acton's shorter titles was *Unmarried Wet-Nurses.*

The Functions and Disorders etc. was strongly recommended by the *Lancet*, which pronounced itself as 'refusing to join in that opinion which regards the consideration of the topics in question as beyond the duties of the medical practitioner'. The book ran to eight editions in Britain and America, and appeared until the end of the century. As a sex manual it was doubly all balls, being nonsense and entirely about males.

Acton draws the clinical picture of the male masturbator:

> The frame is stunted and weak, the muscles
> undeveloped, the eye is sunken and heavy, the
> complexion is sallow, pasty, or covered with spots
> of acne, the hands are damp and cold, and the skin
> moist. The boy shuns the society of others, creeps
> about alone, joins with repugnance in the
> amusements of his schoolfellows. He cannot look
> any one in the face, and becomes careless in dress
> and uncleanly in person.

The donnish type. But Dr Acton perceives: 'His intellect has become sluggish and enfeebled, and if his evil habits are persisted in, he may end in becoming a drivelling idiot or a peevish valetudinarian.'

Acton's additional symptomatology includes pallor, emaciation, slouching, clammy palms, glassy eyes, averted gaze, apathy, amnesia, loss of concentration, no self-reliance, no drive, bad temper, general lunacy, incoherent speech and early death if not forestalled by suicide. This clinical picture is created by the steady leak of semen from the body, though anyone presenting so unattractive a persona would joyfully seize any excuse for it whatever.

Even males pursuing an austere hands-off policy could suffer these alarming symptoms blamelessly through spermatorrhoea. This precipitated nocturnal emissions. The prophylaxis of masturbation itself could be effected by cold baths, use of the dumb-bells, going to bed in metal gloves like kitchen graters, or in a strait-jacket, or by a belt which armoured the penis in a metal mould, or by simply cutting the nerve and anaesthetising the penis for life. Nocturnal emissions could be prevented by an electric alarm applied to the penis, which on erection woke the household with a loud bell, or by a padlocked ring with four sharp spikes, to prickle the expanding flesh (many men might have found this rather nice). The cure was marriage, copulation being symptom-free, though this was restricted by Dr Acton to once a week (for couples living in towns).

Although *The Silent Friend* of 1853 offers minatory drawings of masturbatory sufferers – the slighter cases resembling prim-lipped schoolmasters, the worst having lowered lids, lolling tongue and saliva all over the collar – nobody ever encountered all these symptoms and signs, described so definitely, walking about the streets.

Why such nonsense should be as solemnly propagated by doctors as believed by patients may be explained by comparing masturbatory to masticatory activity. Today, on reasonably sound but not infallible evidence, doctors advise against fatty foods and overeating. This advice is so hungrily grasped by the public, they have generously created a world-wide vastly profitable slimming industry

(Weight Watchers has a turnover of $900 million a year). Everyone trembles at the physical, aesthetic and moral dangers of being in the slightest overweight. This is because everyone has the necessity of feeling guilty about *something*. And a sin stretched universally spins a soft hair-shirt.

Victorian females were known to masturbate, for which the suggested cure was a medieval chasity-belt or surgical removal of the clitoris, but it did not seem to worry anyone very much.

Jack the Ripper

What a captivating Victorian melodrama he stars in! Gas-light, bewhiskered policemen with bull's-eye lanterns, slum alleys, gin, tarts, villains, buckets of blood, enough human organs to stock a butcher's window. Whitechapel! A name with the ring of death, like Tyburn or the Tower. The district is now boringly decorous, bombed and rebuilt in suburban style, embellished by the world-famous Royal London Hospital, and only a stop on the Tube from the edge of the pompous City, where money has lost its vulgarity by becoming a coloured item on a computer screen. The tarts have gone up West and up-market, and the villains now have cars and phones, to free their villainy from the parochial to all of us.

In 1888 – which its contemporaries styled 'the year of the three eights' – Whitechapel was a crammed area of smoking chimney-pots, falling soot and winter's pea-soup fogs. Each grimy rat-running house roofed several discordant families, and a tide of immigrants had been swept from Russia and Poland up the Thames. Its tattered citizens scraped pennies from making toys, gluing up dolls at two-pence-halfpenny a gross, or they risked 'phossy jaw' working in a phosphorus-match factory for twelve shillings a week, or they 'translated' old clothes, or squatted from eight a.m. to nine p.m. in sweatshops, stitching gowns and hats and riding-habits for England's reputable ladies, who thought of such fellow humans only fleetingly, and as of the savages in Africa.

In the Whitechapel streets, the poor sold to the poor. The mutton-pie shops flared cheerfully with gas, the cook shops offered tasty penny saveloys and halfpenny dough puddings, and the stewed eels were delicious. They provided the near penniless with tea at three-farthings a pinch, with bread-and-dripping and with treacle – a boon of rich flavour and cheap price. There were shops for second-hand everything, interrupted with the three brass balls of the pawnbrokers. In the markets in Petticoat Lane, and up by the Great Eastern Railway terminus in Brick Lane, raucous costermongers under hissing naphta sold racing pigeons and shoddy clothes, false teeth and oysters from the barrel, also brass wedding-rings for wives who had pawned the gold one for drink.

The Victorians were tolerant of street traders – the tinkers and knife-grinders, the baked-potato man and the bell-heralded muffin-man, the sixpenny-rabbit man, the barrel-organist with his monkey. The pavement acrobats penetrated Whitechapel, but not the sandwichmen, the inhabitants being too poor to attract either advertising or pickpockets. Most of Whitechapel qualified for 'missionary soup', distributed at midday by the conscience of the higher classes, and every Sunday they marched in the Salvation Army, the Hallelujah Lassies invoking God with tambourines and the brass bands blowing the Devil to Hell with tubas.

The pubs (beer at three-halfpence a pint, gin at twopence a dram) and brothels were numerous enough to satisfy human temptation, which is reined less usually by conscience than by available cash. Along the Commercial Road, its cobbles smeared with squashed horse-dung, its filthy gutters holding dead cats and dogs, came country wains and massive iron-wheeled carts bearing the felled trees of Essex, and the daily herds of cows and sheep to slaughter, while in the opposite direction steaming horses hauled drays of British goods to the docks, for conveyance to the glorious Empire, and to the profitable captive markets of the world.

'We have here the heavy fringe of a vast population packed into dark places, festering in ignorance, in dirt, in moral degeneration, accustomed to violence and crime, born and bred within touch of habitual immorality and coarse obscenity. That is no news to the inhabitants of London,' the *British Medical Journal* chided both sides.

This impoverished, reckless, unenviable district caught the nation's fancy at the end of a cold and rainy August in 1888. A forty-two-year-old prostitute, Mary Ann 'Polly' Nicols, had been murdered in Buck's Row, just north of Whitechapel Tube Station, newly opened in 1884. She was five foot two tall, with greying brown hair and brown eyes and a missing front upper tooth; she was wearing a black straw hat, a brown ulster, a brown linsey-woolsey frock, brown stays, flannel drawers, ribbed black stockings and men's boots; her only possessions were a broken mirror and a comb. She was seen by two Spitalfields market porters who were going to work at four in the morning, lying with her skirts round her waist against a stable door. A policeman unmasking his bull's-eye discovered her throat cut from side to side, and found her body 'as warm as a toasted crumpet'.

The police put Polly Nicols into the black-lacquered, blood-drenched 'shell', which conveyed the unexpected Whitechapel dead to the workhouse mortuary on the public death-cart, drawn by one horse and driven by a pauper. The police had tidily washed the bloodstains off the pavement, to the irritation on his arrival of Chief Inspector Abberline of Scotland Yard, formerly of the Whitechapel Division, whose bafflement by the Ripper continued until his retirement to Bournemouth. On the post-mortem table, Polly's throat wound was found deep enough to have sliced through her carotid arteries and jugular veins, also her windpipe and gullet, even her spinal cord in the cervical vertebrae. A ragged half-moon cut had opened her abdomen from ribs to pelvis, her guts lay outside, still attached to the fan of their membranes, which had been sliced, there were two stab wounds in her vagina, and she had a bruise on each cheek. No one in the night had heard a scream.

Polly Nicols had last been seen as the Whitechapel church clock chimed half past two, drunk, telling her lodging-house keeper she was going to make the money for a night's bed. She raised fourpence, but spent it at the Frying Pan pub in Brick Lane on gin. She was identified by her drawers, property of Lambeth Workhouse. She was the wife of a printer in the Old Kent Road, separated for fourteen years, who identified her body. 'I forgive you for what you did to me now that I find you like this,' he said pathetically.

On Saturday week, 8 September, a bright sunny day, the shell under its shabby black pall arrived again at the mortuary with Mary Anne Chapman. She was another prostitute, a coachman's widow, forty-five, five foot tall, with brown hair, blue eyes and a bulbous nose. She had been found at six in the morning near Brick Lane, in a yard outside a cat's-meat shop, a nightly site of commercial love. Her dirty black skirts were round her waist, her knees everted, her hands uncut defending her face. Her possessions were arranged round her – pennies and farthings, a comb, a twist of paper with some pills. She, too, had been near decapitated, her belly was ripped into

131

three flaps, tugged apart to display an abdominal cavity emptied of her guts, which bloodily decorated her right shoulder. Her uterus, the vault of her vagina and a slice of her bladder had vanished.

Mary Chapman had lodged by Spitalfields Church, and she, too, had wandered out drunk to make money for a bed. She had been seen in the Queen's Head and the Ringers, and at two in the morning talking to a middle-aged man 'of foreign looks' who asked, 'Will you?' to which she answered, 'Yes.' Seventeen people lodged over the cat's-meat shop, but none had heard a scream.

At the inquest in the Working Lads' Institute, Dr Bagster Phillips, who did the post-mortem, testified that such an excision of the uterus, with the cervix intact and the rectum avoided, in one sweep of a knife reckoned to be five inches long, could be accomplished only by a hand practised in surgery. Within hours of this hitting the morning papers, the *Lancet* interviewed an agitated sub-curator of a London hospital pathology museum, who six months earlier had a letter from an American staying at Gresham's Hotel in Dover Street, offering for uteri £20 apiece, if preserved in glycerine instead of the customary formalin, so as to keep them floppy. He required them dispatched to America, where his publishers would present one gratis with each copy of the book he had written on the subject. An ingenious promotion, which could have attached a free amputated foot to a textbook of orthopaedics.

Perhaps the American, snubbed by the curator and with his book doing nicely, had set upon the streets of Whitechapel to collect his own? The *Lancet* decided not, though pompously fearing that the murder might excite animosity towards anatomists and curators, by a public 'ever too ready to cast mud at legitimate research'. The sack-'em-up men Burke and Hare were at it again. It did not occur to the *Lancet* that a sheet of hotel writing-paper and a mischievous medical student could pull a solemn sub-curator's leg.

Sunday 30 September, a cold day with snow in the west, staged the Ripper's double act. 'Long Liz' Stride, forty-five, found at 1 a.m. just off the Commercial Road (throat cut only), and Catherine Eddowes, forty-three, discovered by PC Watkins at 1.45 a.m. in Mitre Square in the City (throat cut, face slashed, nose and right ear gone, snicks on both lower eyelids, abdomen ripped open, liver in three slices, guts round neck, piece of gut in left armpit, no left kidney, ovaries or uterus). Her frock, patterned with daisies and lilies, was round her neck. Neither woman had screamed.

The members of the nearby Socialist Working Men's Club were instantly searched and closely questioned, the body of Long Liz embarrassingly having been discovered by the secretary. The Club was crammed with Russian and Polish *émigrés* enjoying a social evening, who pointed out that the murders had obviously been performed by the Tsar's secret police, to do them discredit.

Catherine Eddowes suffered the bad luck of release from Bishopsgate Police Station at one o'clock that morning, giving a 'Ta-ta, old cock, I'll see you again soon!' to the duty sergeant. She had been locked up since nine, drunk. She was seen at 1.35 near Mitre Square, talking to a man of about thirty with a waxed, pointed moustache, dressed inappropriately for Whitechapel in a pepper-and-salt jacket and deerstalker. 'Two More Horrible Murders in the East End. Dreadful Mutilation of a Woman,' proclaimed the halfpenny broadsheets invitingly, as the country shuddered delightfully over its boiled eggs.

Jack the Ripper had meanwhile named himself in a letter to the newspapers ('I am down on whores and I shan't quit ripping them till I do get buckled. Grand work the last job was'). This was written in red ink, apologetically ('I saved some of the proper red stuff in a ginger-beer bottle over the last job to write with but it went thick like glue and I can't use it'). Jack now wrote to the chairman of the Whitechapel Vigilance Committee 'From hell', sending him half a kidney ('the other piece I fried and ate it was very nise'). The kidney showed Bright's disease: so did the victim's other one. The severed renal artery and vein fitted: the donor was not a mischievous medical student.

Jack achieved leading articles in the *BMJ*: 'He is undoubtedly insane,' it diagnosed unspectacularly. The police recruited bloodhounds – Barnaby and Burgho – but lost them in Hyde Park. Chain-mail and electric batteries were suggested for the Whitechapel unfortunates, to electrocute the Ripper up his knife. Policemen were urged to shave their moustaches and patrol in drag. A disquieting surfeit of respectable ladies volunteered to walk the Whitechapel streets as decoy harlots, while the residents let their rooms for those of the West End to watch hopefully out of the windows. Suspects were arrested and mobbed: 'Leather Apron', a bootmaker owning five keen knives; 'The Mad Pork Butcher'; a City clerk, bringing home in his Gladstone bag the liver for his supper.

The tune of *Here We Go Round the Mulberry Bush* inspired:

Hold your hat and hold your skirt,
Jack the Ripper wants a flirt.
He likes the girls all fat and ripe,
Turns them into butcher's tripe.

He may be a Yid or a sailor lad,
He may be a doctor ever so mad,
He plays with his knife, he plays with his chopper,
He'll never be caught by a London copper.

134

Jack's finale was performed on Friday 9 November, foggy and mild and the day of the Lord Mayor's Show. A rent-collector calling at room No. 13 Miller's Court, Spitalfields (at 4s. 6d. a week), found twenty-five-year-old 'Black Mary' Jane Kelly from Limerick on the bed, with her throat cut to the backbone, no nose, scalped, both breasts on the bedside table, her left arm attached only by its skin, her thigh muscles stripped off and arranged with her nose between the breasts, her abdomen ripped across, guts and liver between the open legs (except for bits draped on the picture-rails), left hand feeling into abdominal cavity, no uterus. She took seven hours to reassemble in the mortuary.

The fire was still warm in the grate, the kettle was burnt through, and her clothes were neatly folded for bed. She was last seen at midnight, drunk. Screams were heard during the night – but screams in Whitechapel were commoner than bird-song in Mayfair. A penniless labourer, with no bed and so trudging the streets all night, reported seeing her at two in the morning with a man in a soft felt hat, drawn over his eyes. He might have been the Ripper: they were having a laugh.

'Dreadful murders of unfortunate women of a bad class,' Queen Victoria shuddered over it all.

Jack ripped no more. The public could ease its attention in the newspapers to Parnell and Kitty O'Shea, the new German Emperor Wilhelm II and *The Yeoman of the Guard* at the Savoy.

Jack Who?

The Victorian police never discovered Jack the Ripper, but many later authors did.

Their suspects, more respected than the contemporary

slaughtermen, butchers, cobblers, mad Russians and doctors with their little black bags, were:

1 Sir William Withey Gull, Bt

Description. Age seventy-one. Physician to Queen Victoria. At Guy's Hospital, a Fellow of the Royal Society, DCL Oxford, LL D Cambridge and Edinburgh, member of the GMC, etc. Cured the Prince of Wales of typhoid in 1871 by masterly inactivity. Short and fat, witty, overbearing, son of an Essex bargee, died in 1890 and left £344,000, a record accumulation for the medical profession, in which he was disliked.

Evidence. He was a Mason, and they get up to peculiar things. He did the Whitechapel murders in a moving carriage, after pressing on the victims poisoned grapes ('Let me peel you a grape, m'dear – What! Never seen one in your life?'). He shortly went mad, and died in an asylum under the name of Mason. His funeral as Sir William was a cover-up, the coffin filled with stones, though the rite attracted Lister, Paget and the medical nobs, and necessitated a special train from Liverpool Street.

Sir William was accused by the artist Walter Sickert and by Robert James Lees, the Queen's spiritualist who called up Prince Albert via John Brown at Windsor. After the double murder in September, Lees recognised Jack the Ripper on a horse-bus at Notting Hill. He dismounted at the same stop, tracked him to Harley Street, denounced him to a policeman as the Ripper – identified by supernatural knowledge – and got a guffaw. Lees persisted, investigated, and discovered him to be Sir William. This is clearly nonsense. Queen's physicians do not hop on a bus, even today.

Defence. In October 1887, Sir William suffered the first of four strokes, afflicting him with right-sided paralysis and loss of speech. He partly recovered, but gave up practice, though naturally remaining on the medical *Register*. He suffered also from severe arthritis.

Verdict. Even if you yearned to spend the night lurking round Whitechapel eviscerating women, in such a physical condition you would have regretfully to forgo it: far preferable a hot toddy, bed, and Robert Louis Stevenson's latest, *The Strange Case of Dr Jekyll and Mr Hyde*.

2 Walter Richard Sickert

Description. The Man Behind the Ripper. Age twenty-eight. Impressionist painter. Danish father, English mother, born in Munich, studied at the Slade, worked with Whistler, a friend of Degas and Toulouse-Lautrec, his *Ennui* in the Tate depicts married life before television.

Evidence. Convenient for Sickert's Bloomsbury studio was a tobacconist's, where 'Black Mary' Kelly (to be the final victim) served behind the counter with Annie Crook, who moonlighted by modelling for him. The Duke of Clarence, 'Prince Eddy', next-but-one heir to the throne, dropped in for a packet of fags while dabbling in the arts (as today's Prince Eddy dabbles in the stage). Eddy fell for Annie, she shortly had a baby girl in Marylebone Workhouse, they later married secretly at St Saviour's, were kidnapped by the Victorian MI5, Annie was sent to a madhouse, and Eddy was sent to his room at Buckingham Palace.

Defence. Mary Kelly sank into Whitechapel vice, and fell in with the Mrs Nichols, Chapman, Stride and Eddowes. They tried blackmailing Prince Eddy, via Sickert. Sickert patriotically reported it to the Prime Minister, the Marquess of Salisbury. It was the Prime Minister who instructed Gull to eliminate the four women, because, as Sickert was constantly warning, the Freemasons ran the country.

Verdict. Fantastic!

3 The Duke of Clarence

Description. Age twenty-four. Prince and Mason.

Evidence. Known by Gull to suffer periodic attacks of erotomania. On a Caribbean cruise with the Royal Navy nine years earlier, these had caused him to attempt the murder of a native woman. He died of pneumonia at Sandringham in 1892, aged twenty-eight, his bluff and non-erotic brother George conveniently taking over both his heirdom and his fiancée Mary. Eddy was rumoured to be officially murdered precisely for these purposes.

Defence and Verdict. One does not do that sort of thing.

4 Montague John Druitt

Description. Age thirty-one. Winchester, Oxford, Inner Temple, became a barrister in 1885, not much good at it, doubled as a schoolmaster at Blackheath, south-east London.

Evidence. His cousin Lionel in Australia said he did it. Sir Melville Macnaughten of Scotland Yard agreed: 'He was sexually insane and from private info I have little doubt but that his own family believed him to have been the murderer.' Druitt's body was hauled from the Thames on 31 December 1888, after a month in the water and less than two since the Ripper stayed his hand.

Defence. Druitt was a keen cricketer. The morning after the Ripper's first murder he was playing cricket in Devon. The very same morning of the second he was batting at home for Blackheath CC at the Rectory Field. The cricket season ended before the Ripper's did. Even the stoutest player of West Indian bouncers would surely have trouble with his strokes after such appalling night-time activities, not to mention suffering bad form from loss of sleep.

Verdict. Not out.

5 James Kenneth Stephen

Description. Age twenty-nine. Poet (light verse). Eton and Cambridge, known as 'JKS'. Became a Fellow of King's, died aged thirty-two.

Evidence. Tutor to Prince Eddy, 1883.

Defence. Not a Mason.

Verdict.

> Will there ever come a season
> Which shall rid us from the curse
> Of a prose that knows no reason
> And an unmelodious verse:
> When the world shall cease to wonder
> At the genius of an Ass,

JKS wrote presciently of the twentieth-century authors who have tipped their loads of illogical rubbish on to the unnamed grave of Jack the Ripper.

An opened abdomen is a confusing medley of slippery tubes and lumps. The uterus, deep in the pelvis, is difficult to lay hands on. The Ripper had some anatomical knowledge, and was perhaps a failed or unbalanced medical student. That the victims did not scream when they saw his knife suggests that he first silenced them with a handkerchief over their mouth and nose soaked in powerful chloroform. If the police noticed the sickly smell, they would reasonably attribute it to drink.

Perhaps Jack the Ripper killed himself after the spectacular in Miller's Court. Or perhaps he simply got tired of it all, and settled down to a life of Victorian respectability.

NINE

The Myth of Feminism

. . . .

An 1884 du Maurier *Punch* cartoon. An elegant party-going pair in evening dress stare across the drawing-room at a younger couple deep in talk.

The Colonel:	'Yes; *He* was senior wrangler of his year, and *She* took a mathematical Scholarship at Girton; and now they're engaged!'
Mrs Jones:	'Dear me, how interesting! and oh, how different their Conversation must be from the insipid twaddle of Ordinary Lovers!'

THEIR CONVERSATION

He:	'And what would *Dovey* do, if Lovey were to *die*?
She:	'Oh, Dovey would die *too*!'

Votes for Women

The lead story in *The Times* on Thursday 5 June 1913:

The race for the Derby yesterday was marked by
two incidents for which it will be long
remembered, not only by the vast gathering at
Epsom, but by all who take an interest in English
sport. The King's horse was brought to the ground
by a woman suffragist, who rushed from the crowd
at Tattenham Corner, apparently with the object of

seizing the reins. The horse fell and rolled on the jockey, who, however, was not severely hurt. The woman was knocked down and received such serious injuries that it was reported at first that she had been killed. The second incident – there has been no parallel to it for about 70 years – was the disqualification of the favourite, Craganour, after the horse had passed the post leading by a neck, and the declaration by the Stewards that the race had been won by Aboyeur, a horse which had been deemed so little worthy of consideration that the odds against it were 100 to 1.

Apart from these occurrences, the one stirring an intense indignation among those who saw it and the other disappointing some thousands of persons who had more than a spectator's interest in the race, there was nothing to deprive the meeting of any of the elements which have hitherto made it a popular festival.

How reassuring this demonstration of the realistic British sense of proportion, only a year before the country needed apply it to the merits of going to war.

It had been a lovely day at Epsom for the 134th Derby. Seventy in the shade, King George V and Queen Mary in the royal box.

The King's horse Anmer was quickly back on its legs, dragging Herbert Jones, its jockey, along the turf by a foot caught in a stirrup. The racegoers burst from the rails, the mounted police galloped up, and a placard arose in the crowd demanding votes for women.

Jones suffered cuts, black eyes and a sore arm, and the next day could go home to Newmarket. The woman was taken unconscious by ambulance to Epsom Cottage Hospital. The staff looked for a fracture of her skull, but found none. They discovered her, from the name-tapes on her clothes, to be a Miss E. W. Davison. Round her waist she wore the colours of the Women's Social and

Political Union – purple, green and white; in her dress pocket was their membership card, a race card and the return half of her ticket from Victoria.

The *Daily Mirror* got the sensational picture of the collision for its next morning's front page, and you could see it all happening in the newsreel that night at the Palace Theatre in the West End. *The Times* set a leader on the theme that suffragettes were all barmy, and the King gave orders to be kept informed of the jockey's condition.

After Derby Day at Epsom came The Oaks. The crowd packed Tattenham Corner in ghoulish anticipation of a rerun disaster. It had been raining heavily immediately before the start, and a runner (Crisp up) gratifyingly tumbled before their eyes. A fortnight later at Royal Ascot, the Gold Cup was disrupted by a man brandishing a suffragette flag and a revolver, bringing down the favourite and injuring himself. He was Harrow and Cambridge and carried a Bible inscribed: 'Oh the weariness of these races and the crowds they attract', and was officially assessed to be unbalanced.

The instigator of the Derby outrage was reported by the Cottage Hospital the day after her admission to be improving and 'able to take some nourishment' – an ironic item in the newspapers, her previous ones being for going on hunger strike.

In 1906, Emily Wilding Davison had joined the suffragettes' Women's Social and Political Union, founded by Emmeline Pankhurst three years earlier. She got two months imprisonment for a disturbance in Limehouse in 1909, went on hunger strike and was released. The same year, she was stone-throwing in Manchester, jailed for two months and forcibly fed ('the hosepipe incident in Strangeways'), then released after eight days.

Her story was repeated in November 1910, when she broke a House of Commons window, and a year later when she got six months for setting fire to pillar-boxes in Westminster with paraffin-soaked rags. She tried to commit suicide by tumbling down the stone staircase in Holloway – forebodingly, because she felt that her cause would be strengthened with a tragedy. In November 1912, she got ten days, annulled after four days' fast, 'for assaulting a Baptist minister by mistake for Mr Lloyd George at Aberdeen'.

The police at Epsom announced that they were doing nothing about Miss Davison. But her condition deteriorated. She relapsed into unconsciousness. The pressure inside her skull was rising, she was clearly bleeding somewhere into her brain. Mr Mansell Moulin, London surgeon and suffragette enthusiast, came to trephine her. She was announced as 'extremely critical'. She died four days after her adventure, at 4.50 in the afternoon on 8 June. Someone on the staff of the Cottage Hospital had earlier missed that she had sustained a fracture running across the base of her skull.

Her female friends had invaded the hospital, erecting a purple, green and white screen round her deathbed. Her brother appeared, Captain RN (ret.). It emerged that Emily Davison was thirty-eight, born in Blackheath, a graduate of London University and with a first in Eng. Lit. at Oxford. She was the most prominent of the militant suffragettes, and now her prominence was presented to the nation.

At the inquest two days after her death, the coroner – after warning 'no politics allowed' – inquired of her naval brother whether she was abnormal mentally, to be told that she was a woman of very strong reasoning facilities. Had she deliberately picked the King's horse? The leading runners racing down the slope to Tattenham Corner were strung out, but the also-rans formed a bunch into which Emily Davison intruded, hands aloft. The coroner decided it was impossible for the dead woman, in a desperate few seconds, to have selected the purple, scarlet sleeves and gold braid of the King's colours. Her fatal intention was to disrupt the race.

After an hour and twenty-five minutes the jury agreed with the coroner, returning a verdict of death by misadventure. The Women's Social and Political Union did not: 'What she did was to challenge the very head of this country, the Government, and the Press with an act that could not be kept out of the papers.' They were determined that she would have a martyr's funeral, ignoring the observation made sixteen years earlier by their predictable supporter George Bernard Shaw: 'Martyrdom is the only way in which a man can become famous without ability.'

The funeral procession the following Saturday from Victoria Station would pass the Union's headquarters in Kingsway, pause for a brief memorial service in Bloomsbury, and reach King's Cross for the 5.30 to Newcastle, which was close to Morpeth, her home. The Commissioner of Police warned them against disrupting the traffic. The open hearse with four black horses was escorted by women in white, the flowers were white, black and purple, the crowd jammed Piccadilly Circus, propaganda leaflets were distributed and there were two bands. They almost missed the train.

Mrs Emmeline Pankhurst had appeared in black at her front door, to be immediately arrested under the 'Cat and Mouse Act', by which a prisoner could be released when ill but rearrested when feeling better. She sent her empty carriage instead. Amid the reverence, someone shouted: 'Three cheers for the King's jockey!' By 1913, people were becoming the tiniest bit tired of the suffragettes.

They had started making a cranky nuisance of themselves – in stolid Edwardian opinion – in the autumn of 1906. The Liberals had swept out the Conservatives, Sir

Henry Campbell-Bannerman was Prime Minister, and the Home Secretary was Herbert Gladstone, who contrasted with his father in supporting the female vote, but was a splintery chip off the old block. The suffragettes disrupted political meetings – 'Couldn't you behave like ladies for once?' demanded the exasperated Lloyd George in the Albert Hall in 1912 – chained themselves to railings, threw stones, smashed windows and raised fires. The Tea Pavilion at Kew, the croquet pavilion at Roehampton, the football pavilion at Cambridge, Yarmouth pier and several lonely railway stations all exhibited their ashes.

At four o'clock precisely on Friday 1 March 1912, every shop window was shattered in Piccadilly Circus, Regent Street and Oxford Street by an assault force with hammers in their muffs. They put bombs in City offices and one behind the Coronation Chair in Westminster Abbey (it was made in a large bicycle bell), and the newspapers hit on calling them 'the Bombazines'. They ruined with acid the greens of fashionable golf clubs, and horrified King George by replacing the flags in the holes of his Balmoral course with those of the Union's colours.

They ripped with cleavers the Rokeby Venus. They slapped the faces of policemen. A Bow Street magistrate, strolling at the weekend on the North Downs, was ambushed and nearly tossed over the White Cliffs by two young women. The reverend Lloyd George lookalike was thrashed by Emily Davison with a dog-whip, a Radical MP was whipped by a woman in mistake for Mr Asquith, the male doctor at Holloway Prison was flogged by three girls with a rhinoceros-hide sjambok (some men might have quite liked all this).

Their ringleader was Emmeline Pankhurst, 'The General', now turned fifty, both daughter and wife of intellectual radicals from Manchester. She was widowed in 1898, and became registrar of births and deaths for the suburb

145

of Rusholme. In 1900, she abandoned this placid job to mount her broom and ride the whirlwind which she had sown with her breakaway Manchester women's suffrage committee. Her twenty-year-old daughter Christabel, spurning a fine, was jailed in 1905 after disrupting an election meeting addressed by Sir Edward Grey (she had required to be kicked hard downstairs by stewards), and the commotion in the newspapers inspired Emmeline that sweet are the uses of adversity, if combined with astute publicity.

In the first three months of 1913, sixty-six suffragettes had gone to jail and eight had been released through hunger strike. If they refused to eat, the prison doctor ran a rubber tube into their stomach via their nose and poured in some nourishing liquid. Such 'forced feeding' was harmless, but denounced by the suffragettes as torture.

Mrs Pankhurst herself was tried at the Old Bailey in 1912 for conspiracy, jailed in Holloway, went on hunger strike and was released. In 1913, she got three years' penal servitude for incitement to violence, adopted the hunger strike but was caught under the Cat and Mouse Act and served thirty days, spread by twelve arrests over a year. She sailed away to raise £4,500 from generous and impressionable Americans, and was rearrested on docking in Plymouth to resume her disjointed sentence.

In 1926, she joined the Conservative party, and stood as their parliamentary candidate for Whitechapel.

The suffragette anarchists were largely upper-middle-class. The votes which they won for women were mostly Conservative ones. They faded from history leaving one glory. Revolutionary movements soon acquire a following of ghouls, but the suffragettes inflicted only one fatal casualty – their Derby Day martyr, poor Emily Davison.

'I am bound to say I think your case has marched backwards,' Home Secretary Winston Churchill was warning them in 1910. Idealistic disruption was achieving only irritation and intolerance. In 1913, the activities of the suffragettes filled eleven and a half double-column pages of the *Times* index. Sir Almroth Wright, chief of the Inoculation Department at St Mary's Hospital, later the champion of Alexander Fleming's penicillin, published a three-column letter in the paper explaining scientifically how half of all middle-aged women went mad. The daughter of the owner of the *Morning Post* suggested: 'When a suffragette has been convicted, first have her well birched (by women), then shave off her hair, and finally deport her to New Zealand or Australia.'

The Great War cracked open the twentieth century. Women drove army lorries, signalled for the Navy, nursed the wounded, made shells and aeroplanes, conducted trams and buses, had a quarter of a million tilling the soil, another quarter of a million becoming Civil Servants, and another filling the jobs of enlisted office workers. Their skirts got shorter, the female munitions workers travelled in trains on workmen's tickets, and stood their round in the pubs. Women showed themselves to be jolly good chaps.

Acts of Parliament

The suffragettes' bedrock argument was: 'Why should women obey laws made by men?'

After Earl Grey's Reform Bill in 1832, a petition for women's votes was presented to Parliament by the Radical MP Henry 'Orator' Hunt, whose encouraging speech to the rioters at Peterloo had got him three years inside. Petitions were sporadically borne to Westminster and oblivion, though in the House in 1866 Mr Disraeli was very kind:

147

In a country governed by a woman, where you allow women to form part of the other estate of the realm – peeresses in their own right, for example – where you allow a woman not only to hold land, but to be a lady of the manor and hold legal courts, where a woman by law may be a churchwarden and overseer of the poor, I do not see, when she has so much to do with the State and Church, on what reasons, if you come to right, she has not the right to vote.

If Queen Victoria was not kind: 'The Queen is most anxious to enlist everyone who can speak or write or join in checking this mad, wicked folly of "Woman's Rights" with all its attendant horrors, on which her poor feeble sex is bent, forgetting every sense of womanly feeling and propriety' she added about its popular protagonist: 'Lady Amberley ought to get a *good whipping*,' nor, later, was Edward VII: 'The conduct of the so-called Suffragettes has really been so outrageous and does their cause (for which I have no sympathy) much harm.'

After 1870, women's suffrage bills were debated in the House of Commons regularly, if pointlessly. Some were passed: in 1870 by 33 votes, in 1886 by a hair's breadth and in 1807 by 71. But they were private members' bills, and Satan was complacently instructed by the Government to 'get thee behind me'.

Women were already permitted to vote in local elections – in 1897, 729,758 of them – to sit as councillors, on school boards and as poor-law guardians nurturing the seeds of the welfare state. In 1910, the suffragettes called a truce. A Conciliation Bill giving women householders the vote was passed by 299 to 186. But Asquith's Government took fright at the substantial opposition, and piled it into Parliamentary amnesia. In January 1918, Lloyd George's Government gave women over thirty the vote without a second thought. What a difference a war makes.

American women kicked up less fuss. They were already feeling their civic oats, and they were unknowing of the exclusively male construction of Victoria's middle-class England. The public schools and Oxford and Cambridge, the clubs in St James's, the Law and the Church were the entitlement of men as unquestionably as the Army and Navy. The upbringing of Englishmen was directed to running the British Empire, and English-women were expected to lie contentedly in their masters' social shadow, like the Oriental ones they ruled.

In American states where women's suffrage stirred, anti-suffrage associations leapt to life (there was only one in Britain, formed in 1909 under the most superior person Lord Curzon and the novelist Mrs Humphrey Ward). This was because American men faced a horror spared the Englishman: women were the temperance sex, and would vote for prohibition. Women lost enfranchisement for a state's elections in 1896 through terror that they would turn California dry.

The American woman got the vote in 1920. French-women had to wait until 1946. In the USSR, women were free to vote in 1917. Australian women had voted since 1902, but the women of New Zealand were the world's most experienced voters, from 1893. In 1928, British women were adjudged to mature as speedily as men, and aged twenty-one were awarded the 'Flappers' Vote' (a flapper, apart from being applied like a cloche hat to a 1920s girl, is a young wild duck, as contributed to *The Natural History of Selborne* in 1789). In that ultimately triumphant year, one militant female needed to confess sadly that feminists were widely seen as 'spectacled, embittered women, disappointed, childless, dowdy, and generally unloved'.

In the parliaments of medieval kings sat the abbesses

of Barking, Shaftesbury, Wilton and Winchester. But British women were not zealous to embody their franchise. The election of December 1918, with thirteen million male voters and eight and a half million female, returned one woman.

Nobody has heard of Britain's first woman MP. She was Countess Markiewicz, formerly Constance Gore-Booth, Irish horse-riding suffragette, who represented South Dublin for Sinn Fein and, like the rest of her party, did not take her seat at Westminster. The second woman MP was returned at a by-election in 1919, Lady Astor, who saw to it that absolutely everybody had heard about *her*. Under 350 women have become MPs at elections since 1918, though they did have a Prime Minister.

The historian A. J. P. Taylor has a curious story. In the two-day debate of 7 May 1940, after the disastrous Norway campaign, Prime Minister Chamberlain was being urged in the House with Cromwellian passion: 'Depart, I say, and let us have done with you. In the name of God, go!' The Labour party shirked forcing a division to back this sentiment, through fear of the Conservatives loyally supporting their leader, however calamitous, and keeping him in office. On 8 May, Labour announced that they *would* divide the house. They seemed to have plucked up courage during the night. But: 'Their hand was forced – a little-known fact – by the women MPs. These had an all-party room of their own, and, in discussion there, resolved to force a vote if no one else did so.'

The government's majority dropped from 240 to 81. The next day, Chamberlain went and Churchill entered. The day after, Hitler's troops poured into Holland and Belgium. Our finest hour was at hand. In gratitude to the First World War for giving them the vote, women saw to it that we won the Second.

The object of this Essay is to explain, as clearly as
I am able, the grounds of an opinion which I have
held from the very earliest period when I had
formed any opinions at all on social or political
matters, and which, instead of being weakened or
modified, has been constantly growing stronger by
the progress of reflection and the experience of life:
That the principle which regulates the existing
social relations between the two sexes – the legal
subordination of one sex to the other – is wrong
in itself, and now one of the chief hindrances to
human improvement; and that it ought to be
replaced by a principle of perfect equality, admitting
no power or privilege on the one side, nor
disability on the other.

So John Stuart Mill in 1869 opened *The Subjection of
Women*, with its first forthright chapter-heading: 'The
Rule of Women by Men is Founded on Brute Force and
on Unthinking Sentiment'.

Like sanitarian Sir Edwin Chadwick, Mill was one of
Jeremy Bentham's young men, who gave the name to
'Utilitarianism' (he had seized the word from a novel by
John Galt, depictor of homely Scottish life). Mill ex-
pounded utilitarianism all his life (with modifications),
and when he became the MP for Westminster in 1865
he expressed the doctrine of 'the greatest happiness of
the greatest number' by voting with the Radicals and
becoming the zealous advocate of women's suffrage.

After thirty-five years in the India Office, and pushing
sixty, John Stuart Mill stood as a Liberal. He was an
admirable candidate, who refused to perform any elec-
tioneering, or to take any interest in local affairs, and
who responded to the angry accusation of writing about
the working class as 'generally liars' with the philosophi-

cal reply 'I did'. He idiosyncratically, and perilously, championed votes for women. Though as a woman's property then passed to her husband on marriage, the only emancipated voters would be widows and spinsters with enough cash to be ratepayers.

Stunned by such intellectual arrogance, Westminster elected him. The newly formed London Suffrage Committee clutched him savagely to their collective bosom. Mill presented to the House a petition with 1,449 signatures, all female, if unfortunately all nonentities. The next year, he proposed an amendment to the Representation of the People Bill, which spread the vote to poorer householders and into the industrial towns.

Mill's argument was that 'man' in the wording included 'woman', as in 'mankind'. He quoted Lord Romilly's Act of 1850, which said as much. The emotional intensity of his speech reduced him to silence for the following two minutes, his eyebrows working furiously. It did not wash. The House did not wish women to win the vote, particularly not through semantics. In 1866, the Westminster voters returned to normal and elected instead W. H. Smith, the newsagent who made a fortune from the railway-bookstall monopoly and achieved laudable fame as a Cabinet minister by becoming W. S. Gilbert's Ruler of the Queen's Navee.

'Would mankind be at all better off if women were free?' asked Mill. 'If not, why disturb their minds, and attempt to make a social revolution in the name of abstract right?' The cradle-rocking classes agreed. They were unimpressed by Mill's concern for them. They wanted contentment, not equality. They were devoutly obeying God's commands by going forth from the schoolroom and multiplying. They expected the male to protect them, if sometimes to exploit them.

The world of Mill's readership was enjoying the novelty of scientific probing. 'Even the preliminary knowledge, what the differences between the sexes now are, apart from all question as to how they are made what they are, is still in the crudest and most incomplete state,' he judged cautiously.

This knowledge was advanced twenty years later by physician Sir James Crichton-Browne, in an oration to the Medical Society of London. Sir James had somehow got the idea that the blood supply to that part of the brain responsible for intelligent decision and analytic thought was richer in men, but in women the blood flowed stronger to the bit handling emotions. And anyway, women's brains were too light for intellectual use.

Men were then as fancifully obsessed with the size of women's brains as later with that of their bosoms. Mill wrote decisively about Cuvier, the French anatomist who became a Cabinet minister: 'It is within my knowledge that a man who has weighed many human brains. said that the heaviest he knew of, heavier even than Cuvier's [the heaviest previously recorded], was that of a woman.' Girls should not overtax an inadequate brain by such things as learning logarithms, Sir James warned. He exemplified some female students whom he had shiveringly encountered with 'stooping gait and withered appearance, shrunk shanks, and spectacles on nose'. Better stick to boiling potatoes.

Apart from those differences universally recognised for exercising multiplication, the physical contrasts between men and women are unexciting.

1 The pelvis. The gynaecoid pelvis is broader, shallower and rounder than the android, a basin rather than a funnel. This difference, evident even from a fragment, is useful in determining the sex of bodies dug up by archaeologists or the police.
2 Women have less muscle than men, and more fat under

the skin. Fat distribution is different: on the hips and thighs rather than on the belly as in males.

3 The pubic hair. In women, the top edge is horizontal, if sometimes reaching upwards towards the umbilicus, like a man's.

4 The carrying angle. Women being pear-shaped, with wider hips than men's, have a wider outward angle at the elbow – arms by the side, palms facing the front – than do men. This might be interpreted as a Darwinian provision for carrying a pair of shopping-baskets.

5 Gap between the legs. Female athletes sprinting towards the television camera show a gap between their legs, which are further apart because of the shape of their pelvis. Male thighs are closer despite the scrotum.

6 Women live longer than men. They are more resistant to many illnesses, and since Professor Domagk's sulpha drugs started minimising puerperal fever just before World War Two, it has become rare for women to die in childbirth. The maternal mortality rate was 4.3 per thousand births in 1935. Now there are only forty-five deaths a year in England from all complications of pregnancy.

7 Males have a higher mortality *in utero* and in infancy.

8 Males have in their blood testosterone, a hormone produced in the testis by the interstitial cells named after Franz von Leydig, anatomist of a century ago. Young men have it bounding in their arteries, but the blood level drops to half at the age of fifty. Women, too, have a little testosterone, produced by their adrenal glands.

9 This endocrine difference accounts for women being less aggressive than men. This may be proved conclusively by the experiment of driving for twenty minutes along any motorway.

10 Women have the ability to shine in the careers that men do, but seldom reach the top. This is another effect of their natural paucity of testosterone, and thus lack of the essential aggression to mount the final jostling steps.

11 'It cannot be inferred to be impossible that a woman should be a Homer or an Aristotle, or a Michael Angelo, or a Beethoven, because no woman has yet actually

produced works comparable to theirs in any of those lines of excellence,' argued John Stuart Mill. Women are more artistic than men. Their failure to become great artists is another fault of women's worthy testosterone-deficient unaggressiveness. It is not the fault of the testosterone-stuffed predominantly male critics.

Menstruation, copulation, gestation, parturition, nutrition, elevation – women operate the mechanics of multiplication from puberty to menopause. These became more tedious to bear with the advancing and inviting complexity of civilisation. 'The male clerk with his quill pen and copperplate handwriting had gone for good,' wrote A. J. P. Taylor of 1918. 'The female short-hand-typist took his place. It was a decisive moment in women's emancipation.'

It was daughterly emancipation. The typewriter was the weapon of women's liberation from the family home. The bicycle was its vehicle. A chaperone, a watchful parent, was left behind by such unequivocally solitary transport. You pedalled away with the man of your choice (a Chaperone Cyclists' Association was desperately founded in 1896, but never caught up). Eve was spinning everywhere. In the early 1890s, only two bikes in a hundred were bought by women; by the mid-1890s they took a third of the output.

Bloomers was its uniform. Cycling, unlike riding or tennis, could not be performed in sweeping skirts. Amelia Jenks, a handsome girl from Homer in New York State, when twenty-two in 1840 had married Mr Bloomer and started a perky women's magazine, *The Lily*. Bored with cumbersome dresses, she designed for herself and her readers a startling 'Walking Costume', a purple and white silk dress which extended only two inches below the knee, revealing matching silk trousers which were gathered tightly at the ankles, round the prunella uppers of her boots. 'They style of the trousers may be described as Turkish,' she said. Why, for the first time you could see that a woman's legs moved when she walked. By 1896, bloomers had become knickerbockers reaching to knee-socks, with pockets to stick your hands in, worn below a belted jacket and topped by the fashionable boater. This was the 'Rational Costume', its complications observed by *Punch*:

> *The Vicar of St Winifred-in-the-Wold (to fair Bicyclists)*: 'It is customary for Men, I will not say *Gentlemen*, to remove their Hats on entering a Church!'
> *Confusion of the Ladies Rota and Ixiona Bykewell.*

There is an ever-shifting superficial relationship between men and women, modified by the world's inventions, conventions and fashions. Many women now do men's jobs and strike men's attitudes. Many others feel comfortably that the woman's place is in the home, which contains the telephone and the television. And motherhood remains a valuable service to society (priced at about £20 a week by the British government, going by its child allowances).

Evolution is a leisurely manifestation of science. We are biologically the same as the original readers of John Stuart Mill. The feminist evangelists whose shrieks reverberate in the present air can safely fall mute. They have nothing to lose but the golden chains which attach them to their worshippers. Whatever the possible alternative dignifications, we are all sex objects. Were we not, there would be no more us to complain about it.

TEN

Sex Heil!

. . . .

> Hitler . . . has only got one ball!
> Göring . . . has two, but rather small.
> Himmler . . . is somewhat similar,
> But little Göbbels . . . has no balls at all!
> Song to the tune of *Colonel Bogey*, popular in Britain in 1940

. . . .

Hitler's Secret Weapon

For once, a rousing wartime rumour was right:

> Urogenital system: Right testicle only present. No
> evidence of an undescended testicle in left
> inguinal canal.

The medical examination was conducted in November 1923, in Munich prison. Hitler was aged thirty-four, 1.76 metres tall, weighed 76 kilograms, had a pulse of 72 and a blood pressure which rose abnormally when he became excited. His nasal septum was deviated to the right and he suffered from sinusitis, giving him a post-nasal drip of pus; he had eczema on his left shin and boils on the back of his neck, but was otherwise healthy. He was complaining of a painful right shoulder, incurred by falling to the ground to escape being shot by the police.

The accident had occurred in Munich – the Nazi

snake-pit. On the morning of 9 November, Göring and General Ludendorff (reliably victorious, but it was he who had ordered the German government to seek the 1918 Armistice and had dethroned the Kaiser) marched behind the swastika flag at the head of three thousand *Sturmabteilung*. These were the storm troopers, a title dignifying a regiment of rootless ex-soldiers, layabouts and roughnecks, the Brownshirts, though muffled against that bleak morning in anoraks and Norwegian ski-caps. They had assembled in the fenced gardens of the spacious Bürgerbräukeller, where waitresses at rough wooden tables served the splendid Bavarian beer in hefty lidded mugs. The men were armed with carbines, flaunted a lorry with machine-guns, and marched across the River Isar and through the central Marienplatz towards the Bavarian War Ministry on the far side of the city.

It was the start of the national revolution. The march would continue victoriously onward from Munich to Berlin. Hitler had said as much inside the beer hall the evening before.

Ernst Röhm, later to command the brownshirted SA, had during the night seized the local Army Headquarters at the War Ministry with his own batch of storm troopers. But he had overlooked occupying the telegraph room, and had been surrounded since dawn by the German Army, acting on orders wired back from Berlin.

The route to relieve their besieged comrades lay through a narrow street beside the Feldherrnhalle (cribbed from a Florentine palace), blocked at the end by a hundred policemen armed with rifles. A Nazi shouted at the police not to shoot – their party included His Excellency Ludendorff, it would be most improper and impolite. Hitler had a revolver, which he had been brandishing repeatedly over the past twenty-four hours, had fired into the Bürgerbräukeller ceiling, had threatened to kill himself with, and on the march kept waving excitedly. He yelled impatiently: 'Surrender! Surrender!' and fired. The police fired back. In a minute, there were sixteen Nazis and three police dead, Göring wounded and Hitler flat on the pavement. Only General Ludendorff, who was wearing a black overcoat and top-hat (he was retired, and happened to live near Munich), stayed on his feet and with his adjutant walked contemptuously through the police into the open Odeonsplatz beyond.

Hitler fled. The *putsch* was a flop. The 'Beer Hall Revolution' became a national joke. The National Socialist party was dissolved, Hitler was arrested. The mark stabilised, the wartime allies lent Germany 800 million gold marks, and everyone thought that the Nazis would fade away like other freaks evoked by the Weimar Republic.

Hitler was charged with high treason. 'Given a marketplace and an empty barrel, he may be relied upon to gather and enthral an unsophisticated audience,' a British ambassador once noted admiringly. Failure in the Munich streets had not cost him the knack, and he transformed a courtroom ordeal into a magnificent publicity exploit. The oratorical justification of his martyred revolution, performed before the newspapers of the world, abruptly turned Hitler into a national luminary and an international shadow.

On 1 April 1924, the judges found him guilty. The sentence under the law was life imprisonment, but they thought that five years would do. This permitted parole after six months, and Hitler was home for Christmas. He had served time in a comfortable room in the ancient fortress of Landberg, which has delightful views, occupying himself by dictating *Mein Kampf* to Rudolf Hess.

Hitler had been passed fit to stand trial by the Munich prison doctor, who incidentally recorded his genital deficiency. This was the effect of an intra-uterine accident.

The testes have an active prenatal existence. They bud in the male embryo on either side of the evolving backbone, on the level of the lower ribs. Each undergoes a curious passage during pregnancy through the developing abdomen, dragging its arteries and nerves behind it from the thorax, directed by the *gubernaculum testis* – the 'rudder', though more accurately a tow-rope of muscle fibres secured to the developing scrotum. During the seventh month of pregnancy the testis leaves the abdomen completely, traversing the inguinal canal which runs along the groin to settle cosily in its dangling nest.

Sometimes the journey goes astray. A testis may get stuck in the inguinal canal, or like Hitler's be left wallowing about uselessly half-way down the abdomen. The defect would have stayed secret for life had he not revolted imprudently and been imprisoned, because Hitler was a difficult patient who refused to remove his clothes for examination by his doctors. A man as infamously neurotic as Hitler who possessed only one testis – though he was fertile and sexy, one testis will do – might harbour feelings of inadequacy and resentment against the bulk of mankind who are fully equipped. But his lifetime performance suggests that he felt himself so magnificently unique in the world that he could have been furnished with three.

Dictatorial Sex

On the Saturday night of 16 September 1905, sixteen-year-old Hitler got drunk for the only time in his life. He had left for good his high school at Steyr, in the middle of Austria, which he felt – with reason – did not appreciate him. He was discovered by a milkmaid at dawn, lying in a country ditch. He told the story himself after (a non-alcoholic) dinner during one of his reminiscent evenings amid his long-suffering entourage in the Second World War. He vowed never again to touch a drop, he was a non-smoker and later a vegetarian, but he was not averse to a bit of *Mieze* (pussy).

As a pasty, shy, gawky teenage school-leaver with a nasty temper, Hitler fancied blonde blue-eyed Stefanie of Linz, on the Danube, where he loafed about in a cheap flat with his widowed mother and his sister Paula. He would eye Stefanie, who was older and had been two years at college in Munich and Geneva, while she was out shopping with her own widowed mother. He wrote her reverent love poems which he read insistently to his friend August, an upholsterer, but he never presented them to Stefanie, nor spoke to her, nor tried to meet her. A young man may prefer to let his fancy lightly turn to thoughts of love rather than risk the savage humiliation of rebuff through his own unattractiveness.

By 1929, Hitler had flourished into a ripened politician. The ban on the Nazi party, on its newspaper the *Völkischer Beobachter* (editor: Hitler), even on his addressing public meetings, had all been dissolved by a Bavarian government which deluded itself that sixteen corpses and their leader's six months in Landberg Castle had tamed the disorderly men from the beer hall. Hitler had survived his two years of enforced public silence by redirecting his overpowering oratorical energy into reorganising the National Socialist Party.

His idea was to structure a Nazi state within the German state. He sectioned the Reich into thirty-odd *Gaue*, which were split into *Kreise*, which were divided into *Ortsgruppen*, which were sliced into parcels of streets, which were fragmented into blocks of houses. Each unit had its dedicated leader. The Nazi party became inescapable.

The party created its own departments to match the

Government departments – though with an additional one, to organise the Government's overthrow. In October, Hitler made twenty-nine-year-old propagandist Joseph Göbbels the Gauleiter of Berlin. That January, he had appointed Bavarian chicken-farmer Heinrich Himmler head of the SS – the *Schutzstafel*, Hitler's expanding two-hundred-strong bodyguard, who swore loyalty to him to the death and were dressed in the modish black uniforms of Mussolini's fascists.

Hitler had then turned forty. He possessed the social position and the money to rent a summer villa, the Haus Wachenfeld, in the Obersalzberg above Berchtesgaden. It was his first home of his own. The house was desirably situated near the border, for flight to Austria should the Bavarians decide to arrest him again: though Hitler had renounced his Austrian nationality on 7 April 1925 – to mutual satisfaction – and was one of the stateless citizens whom he was to create innumerably among the refugees from his rule. When he became Chancellor in 1933 he rebuilt the villa lavishly and renamed it the Berghof, and it became world famous through his entertaining there the statesmen of Europe, including Britain's Mr Chamberlain for tea on 15 September 1938, before his squirming signature of the Munich Agreement.

'At this period I knew a lot of women,' Hitler rambled on, one blacked-out evening in 1942. 'Several of them became attached to me. Why, then, didn't I marry?' His feeble excuse was the possible abandonment of a wife through return to a Bavarian jail. 'I therefore had to renounce certain opportunities that offered themselves,' he added intriguingly. 'What lovely women there are in the world! In my youth in Vienna, I knew a lot of lovely women!'

The world's lovely women included his chauffeur's sister Jenny (he spent half the night with her, but only talking in cafés); willowy Erna, the sister of his friend

Putzi Hanfstaengl (a Harvard man, who lent him a thousand dollars); and Wagner's stately brunette daughter-in-law, the widowed Winifred (Hitler sat through *Die Meistersinger von Nürnberg* for over a hundred performances, according to Göbbels). There was an earlier woman experienced in a cowshed, but at the critical moment something went amiss, and passion ended in an overturned milk-churn.

At Berchtesgaden Hitler needed a housekeeper, and conveniently gave the job to his widowed half-sister Frau Raubal, who brought with her from Vienna two daughters, Friedl and Geli. Geli was a twenty-year-old blue-eyed blonde with a nice smile, a simple girl who wanted to be a singer. 'Uncle Alf' fell for her. He treated her to long walks in the mountains, and to sitting through all his meetings. Through his passion, he lapsed into two activities he had always shunned: being seen alone with a woman in public, and going on a picnic. He took a smart flat at 16 Prinzregentenplatz in Munich and installed Geli with the intention of marrying her.

Like many other humans, Geli grew unenthusiastic about Hitler's intentions. He forbade her to be seen with other men. He reluctantly let her go dancing, but only until eleven p.m. and then chaperoned by an ex-sergeant major. He furiously suspected that she was having it off with his bodyguard, the ex-clockmaker and ex-convict Emil Maurice. To her greater distress, he banned her singing lessons. Now she would never appear in *Die Meistersinger*. Why, the man was behaving like a tyrant.

Hitler meanwhile continued courting the lovely women. *On dit* he was going to marry Winifred Wagner instead. He and Geli had rows. Hitler declared that his patience was now at an end, as it was to be famously seven years later towards Czechoslovakia. He lost his temper, cursed her like a navvy and locked her in. The affair seeming to be over, Geli said she was going home to Vienna to stay with a friend and resume her singing career. Hitler forbade her. On 17 September 1931, he was going to Hamburg. Geli called down from a window of the flat: 'Then you won't let me go to Vienna?' He repeated from the car: 'No!' She did not seem particularly upset. She announced to the neighbours that she was going back to mother in Berchtesgaden. She had her dead canary Hansi, lying on cotton-wool in a box which she was carrying around, which she intended to bury up at the villa. She sang a little and wept a little and wrote a commonplace letter to someone in Linz, and the next morning she was found shot dead.

The official verdict was suicide. She was buried in consecrated ground in Vienna, the Catholic Church giving her the benefit of fatal mental confusion. Hitler wept over her grave. Her death had rendered him suicidal for two days. He decided in her memory to become a vegetarian. Geli's room at Berchtesgaden remained untouched, even by the afternoon when Mr Chamberlain called. Her portraits in the Chancellery at Berlin were flower-swathed on the day of her birth and death.

The coroner's report stated that the bullet had entered her chest below the left shoulder and penetrated vertically to the heart. An odd track. Was she really murdered, as a dangerous encumberance, by the conscientious Himmler?

After moving into the Munich flat, Hitler wrote Geli a letter expressing his desire to be dominated and beaten by her, to be smeared with her faeces and splashed with her urine. Coprophilia and undinism are unharmful psychological quirks, Mr Norris was changing trains in 1935, and Miss Whiplash is today as familiar around Piccadilly Circus as Eros. Perhaps Hitler did enjoy a bit of fladge in the evenings. But Hitler wanted, and needed, to appear abnormally virtuous towards women. Such oddities might disastrously make him seem merely human.

The letter to Geli, like the love poems to Stefanie, was never sent. But Hitler unwisely left it lying about the Munich flat, to be pocketed by the landlady's son, Dr Rudolph, who sensed that he had something profitable for the newspapers. Hitler had told Geli about the letter. After he had stopped her going to Vienna she told other people. The Nazi party took fright. The letter was bought – before Geli's death – from Dr Rudolph by an intermediary, Father Bernhard Stempfle of the Order of St Jerome. He specialised in anti-Semitic journalism, and had become friendly with Hitler while copy-editing *Mein Kampf*.

It was a complicated deal. The priest was a friend of an odd dwarf, J. F. M. Rehse, who in Munich collected political memorabilia, from official decrees to leaflets and posters. The Nazi party treasurer, Franz Xavier Schwarz, asked Fr Sempfle to buy the letter off Dr Rudolph, on the excuse that so precious a document would embellish Rehse's collection. Fr Sempfle agreed only if Hitler purchased the entire collection cramming Regse's flat, and appointed the pair of them its curators. The Nazi party was skint at the time, and its faithful scratched their heads at Hitler buying a collection of old posters. Schwarz had to find another hefty sum for Sempfle to pay Dr Rudolph, before he could pass the letter back to Hitler. Geli still talked about it. So did Fr Sempfle. On 30 June 1934, 'the Night of the Long Knives', in the Forest of Harlaching near Munich, Fr Sempfle had his neck broken and three shots in his heart, fired by an SS squad under Emil Maurice.

Eva Braun was another blue-eyed blonde, the middle daughter of a manual worker at Simbach, which is by the Austrian border on the River Inn. She liked swimming, skiing and dancing, and she had quite nice legs (according to Field Marshal Keitel). At twenty-one, she was a shop assistant in Munich for Hitler's photographer Heinrich Hoffmann. Hitler appraised her a nice, quiet girl, he dated her, brought her flowers and kissed her hand, then with the enthusiasm of a misguided Cinderella she told everyone that the prince was going to marry her. Hitler got cold feet, to which she responded in the summer of 1932 by trying to kill herself. Hitler decided in alarm that to lose one girl-friend thus could attract sympathy, but two within a year would raise eyebrows. He moved Eva into the villa at Berchtesgaden, a tactlessness which infuriated his housekeeper, who was Geli's mother.

'A highly intelligent man should take a primitive and stupid woman. Imagine if on top of everything else I had a woman who interfered with my work! In my leisure time I want to have peace,' he later explained patiently to an intimate group, which included Eva herself. He did not want witty or intelligent women about him, he added, in her favour. 'I could never marry,' he expanded. 'Think of the problems if I had children! The chances are slim for someone like me to have a capable son,' he admitted modestly. 'That is almost always how it goes in such cases. Consider Goethe's son – a completely worthless person! Lots of women are attracted to me because I am unmarried. That was especially useful during our days of struggle,' he ended practically.

Nobody in Germany knew about Eva Braun. She shifted between the Munich flat and the Berchtesgaden villa in Hitler's trail, with his two secretaries. She travelled not in Hitler's special train but by the usual express. She seldom got to Berlin, and during the glittering dinners and parties she was kept in her room – which was next to Hitler's bedroom, with a communicating door – reading the latest novels, or she watched films in the private cinema.

Eva was not allowed to mix socially even with the Görings, though when her sister Gretl married Himmler's chief SS man at Hitler's HQ she could be produced occasionally as his sister-in-law. Hitler once gave Eva a week's holiday with the Speers (Albert Speer was his armaments minister and architect; he got twenty years at Nürnberg and died on a trip to London). They took her to Zürs, a pretty skiing village in the Tyrol near the Swiss border, where Speer noted: 'There, unrecogniscd, she danced with great passion into the wee hours of the morning with young army officcrs.' Otherwise, she could dance with, or even chat with, other men only as secretly as she could smoke a cigarette, Hitler disapproving of all three activities.

Hitler now had command of the world's lovely women: in the spring of 1939, he entertained 'tender feelings for a beautiful girl. She is twenty years old, with beautiful quiet eyes, regular features and a magnificent body. Her name is Sigrid von Lappus. They see each other frequently and intimately,' recorded Count Ciano, Mussolini's randy foreign minister.

Eva was Hitler's lady in waiting. He would disappear on his bustling political business leaving her at the Berghof, and during the war he renounced social life to be mostly imprisoned in his eastern or western headquarters. His sex life was that of a travelling salesman from the *petits bourgeois*, which both of them were. Their communicating bedroom door frames visions of intimacy: Did he wear striped pyjamas? Did he fart in bed, on his vegetarian diet? Did he snore much? Have morning erections? How about contraception? No mention of it in the diaries of his personal physician, the obese Theodor Morell. Can we imagine Hitler peeling on a condom?

Eva's political influence on Hitler is assessed minor, but was inescapably major even if supportive, like that of any enduring mistress. Sharing a pillow is sharing power: a man is as indiscreet in his copulation as he is in his cups. Hitler esteemed his dumb blonde as more than a sexual convenience. Speer tells of a tea-time with Eva late home from skiing, Hitler looking nervously at the clock, just like a normal human, uneasy that she had suffered an accident. Hitler bleakly assessed their cosy relationship in his will as 'many years of true friendship', but he must have loved her, because on his last day alive he married her.

If Hitler's habits were trying for a mistress, so they were for everyone else. 'It is always Hitler who talks!' complained Magda Göbbels about his after-dinner conversations which overflowed into the night. 'He repeats himself and bores his guests!' Never a regular worker and as nocturnal as Dracula, Hitler demanded his conferences at night. 'Every night till six or seven in the morning, you could see the light shining from his windows,' recorded Magda's husband reverently. 'The Führer was dictating his great speeches.' Hitler was not woken before nine-thirty a.m. and always shaved himself – he could not tolerate anyone, even his personal hairdresser August Wollenhaupt, laying a razor on his throat, and quite rightly. He also ate a lot of sweets.

Magda, who was rich and stylish, hated Hitler's *Tschapperl*, his dim sweetheart. Eva demanded a deference from Hitler's intimates which Magda refused to bestow. She resented Eva's personal insinuations which incited Hitler to distribute disgrace: the two women got their clothes from the top couturier Romatzki, but when

Magda remarked how insignificant Eva managed to look in them, this did not go over well when relayed to Hitler. 'He is not enough of a man to be able to stand a real woman near him,' Magda concluded, with estimable mortal bitchiness.

Till Death Us Do Part

The Third Reich ended on a Shakespearian note, in a suicidal shambles.

The German Army fought gallantly to the end – it had no option, the Allies having unusually, for both nations or persons, learned by their mistakes. For Peace, Woodrow Wilson's pious Fourteen Points proposed in 1917 was replaced by Winston Churchill's forthright Unconditional Surrender which was bravely, if prematurely, demanded in 1940.

At dawn on 22 April 1945, Russian artillery at Zossen, to the south of Berlin, were firing heavily into the Tiergarten and in the gardens of the ministry buildings along the Wilhelmstrasse. The noise was so violent, it woke Hitler in the Führerbunker thirty feet below the Chancellery, at the early hour of nine a.m. The morning before, he had suddenly appeared unshaven, asking unbelievingly: 'Are the Russians that close?' Now he called a military conference at noon, after his breakfast and his injection by Dr Morell – vitamins, spiked with amphetamine, which he had been receiving up to five times daily, since he had started seriously playing European politics by reoccupying the Rhineland in 1936.

The Führerbunker had thirty cramped bedrooms, they ate in the passages, there was a butler's pantry and a dog-run up in the Chancellery garden. Hitler and Eva Braun occupied five rooms in one corner. The conference was held in the passage, to be told by the Chief of Staff that Russian tanks were overrunning the suburbs, and that the troops defending Berlin along the River Oder to the east were trapped. According to Hitler's valet (an SS man), Hitler threw his coloured pencils across the map-strewn table, took a deep breath and shrieked: 'This is the end! The war is lost!' He added that rather than leave Berlin he would put a bullet through his head, and left. Field Marshal Keitel screamed: 'We have to stop the Führer!' The valet recalled: 'The chaos was indescribable. Some poured themselves brandy from the bottle that stood on the table.' Hitler phoned Göbbels, summoning him to the Führerbunker from his air-raid shelter at home, and to bring Magda and the children. There were six: Helga, aged twelve; Hilde, aged eleven; the only boy, Helmut, aged nine; Holde, aged seven; Hedda, aged six; and Heide, aged four.

There followed a week which must have made *The Twilight of the Gods* look like *A Night at the Opera*.

On Saturday 28 April, Hitler summoned his intimates, repeated that he would kill himself and urged them to follow his example, emphasising his advice by handing round small glass capsules of cyanide. All agreed heartily, though most had second thoughts and fled the Bunker after Hitler's death. SS General Fegelein fled before it, was recaptured on Hitler's orders, in civvies waiting for the Russians, was taken into the Chancellery garden and shot – despite being the husband of Eva Braun's sister.

On Sunday, the Russians were a kilometre away and their firing shook the Bunker violently. The Göbbels children were frightened, and wanted to run away, too, but Mummy wouldn't let them.

That night, Hitler married Eva Braun. It was an act so monstrously incongruous that he must have decided there was no point any longer in remaining unhuman.

Somebody found a registrar in a local unit of the

German Dad's Army, who shook throughout the ceremony. Hitler and Eva affirmed that they were of Aryan descent and had no hereditary diseases. Göbbels returned the compliment of fourteen years earlier and was best man. They held a reception, Hitler had a glass of champagne, but nobody managed to wish them the best of luck. Hitler made two wills and conducted a Cabinet reshuffle: he fired as Nazi traitors, though without doing them any good with their conquerors, Göring (who died of cyanide before the Allies could hang him), Himmler (who died of cyanide, vomiting over a British officer's trousers) and Ribbentrop (who was hanged). Hitler appointed Göbbels Chancellor of the Third Reich.

The next afternoon, Hitler heard that Mussolini was dead: he and his mistress had been shot by partisans in Como while trying to escape to Switzerland, and exhibited the reversal of Fascism's powerful pompousness by hanging upside down outside a filling-station. The next day, 30 April, Hitler threw a farewell lunch and at six o'clock he and Eva killed themselves with cyanide. In the Bunker was his German shepherd, Blondi: 'The dog remained the only living creature at headquarters who aroused any flicker of human feeling in Hitler,' Speer had noticed. He added: 'I avoided, as did any reasonably prudent visitor to Hitler, arousing any feelings of friendship in the dog.' Treacherous even to his dog, Hitler had ordered its trainer to feed it a cyanide ampoule in the lavatory to see if they worked. Henchmen attempted to burn both human bodies to cinders in the Chancellery garden, but like most people in the wartime world they were short of petrol.

The post-mortems on Herr and Frau Hitler were performed by Soviet pathologists on 8 May in the mortuary of a commandeered hospital in Berlin. Their cause of death was cyanide poisoning: Hitler's more military suicide by gunshot was a legend, the Russian pathologist found glass splinters of the capsules in their mouths, and caught the characteristic smell of bitter almonds. He died like his dog.

The Munich prison doctor's observation was confirmed: 'In the scrotum, which is singed but preserved, only the right testicle was found. The left testicle could not be found in the inguinal canal.'

Both Hitlers were identified by their teeth. Adolf's were bad and elaborately engineered; they are kept in a laboratory jar in Moscow. Now that the Berlin wall has vanished, a reluctantly uniting western Europe could be warned of the pains of national divisions by a plinth in Brussels inscribed: 'Here are Hitler's teeth. Don't let them bite again.'

Joseph Göbbels was Reich Chancellor for one day; at nine the next evening he and Magda killed themselves with cyanide. The Russian pathologists noted that Göbbels had a right club foot, the leg 4.4 cm shorter than the left and wearing a brace, that Magda had small breasts, and so did Eva Hitler. Also, that young Helga Göbbels that night was wearing a light-blue nightie trimmed with lace, had pubic hair and an intact hymen, and that her brother Helmut had a green-and-red flower pattern on his white pyjamas.

On the late afternoon of 1 May, Göbbels asked Dr Helmut Kunz, who was detailed from the SS medical branch to be Chancellery dentist: 'Doctor, I would be most grateful if you could help my wife to put the children to sleep.' Magda told them: 'Children, don't be afraid, the doctor is going to give you an injection, a kind that is now given to all children and soldiers.' Dr Kunz administered a dose of morphine into their arms and they were asleep in ten minutes. At twenty to nine, Magda watched Dr Stumpfegger, who was Hitler's doctor after Morell had sagely fled to the Americans, crush a capsule of cyanide in all their mouths. Dr Kunz had refused to. He had earlier offered Göbbels to shelter the children at the military hospital and put them into the care of the Red Cross.

The children of Göring, the ten children of Hitler's powerful secretary Martin Bormann, Himmler's daughter Gudrun and the children of all the top Nazis grew into unmolested, if reflective, maturity. But Göbbels disagreed with Dr Kunz's salvation: 'That's not possible; after all, they are the children of Göbbels!'

The evil that men do lives after them, often with good reason.

Strength Through Joy

Strength Through Joy was Hitler's apparatus to manage the leisure of the German people, so as – he said – to keep them strong enough in mind and body to implement his international policies. It was run by Dr Robert Ley (who hanged himself with his towel in his cell, while awaiting trial at Nürnberg). It provided cut-rate theatre, seemly music-hall, concerts, education, sports, social evenings, tours to German resorts, cruises to Norway and Italy, and the Volkswagen. Its custom-built white cruise ships seldom provided runs ashore, but offered incessant shipboard activities, and had plain-clothes Gestapo men to keep an eye on things. Such mass amusements created a regimented feeling of togetherness, of absorption into the hallowed 'national community' which the Nazis substituted for private life, of *Ein Volk, ein Reich, ein Führer*.

Strength Through Joy could equally have been the motto of the Nazi organisers of the nation's sex.

Hitler himself was presented by his propagandists as superior to sexual desire as the evangelists presented Jesus. His public attitude towards women was one of pompous prudery, though his more raffish colleagues, like Göbbels, generously championed a laxity in sexual morals which faintly reflected their own. But the Germans enjoy an infinite capacity for adulation, and German women worshipped Hitler beyond official requirements. Almost half the Nazi votes in the crucial 1930 election were from women, who had just been enfranchised by the Weimar Republic. They mobbed him with flowers on his egotistical tours of inspection. They showered him with love letters as joyously as the blonde maidens in white dresses who scattered rose-petals before his Mercedes in midsummer 1940 – when the war was over, apart from the inconvenience of the defiant British. On Hitler's birthday, which was celebrated like a combination of the fourth and fourteenth of July, they overwhelmed him with gifts, mostly hand-knitted.

The Nazis peppered the calendar with rousing anniversaries, and ruled Germany through a hundred organisations. Each had a hierarchy of leaders incandescent with enthusiasm, if seemingly insane. They ranged from the Gestapo and the SS to the Men's Association for the Control of Immorality and the Centre for Runology and Emblematology. To oversee sex was the function of the Advisory Board for Population and Racial Policy.

To the Nazis, sex was buxom blonde women producing blonde children, preferably four. This was primarily performed for the gratification of the Führer, not of the family, and he expressed his appreciation with the *Mutterkreuz*: four children won the bronze cross, six the silver, eight was going for gold. This grotesquerie was ceremoniously bestowed on rows of mothers furnished with nosegays on the birthday of Hitler's own (bronze) mother. 'Marriage cannot be an end in itself, but must serve the one higher goal, the increase and preservation of the species and the race. This alone is its meaning and its task,' Hitler put it squarely.

Impatience for family life was first urged in the German Girls' League, which had a dowdy uniform of white blouse and black skirt. 'Your body belongs to your nation,' was the leading advice on health from its medical officer. Ten-year-olds were toughened for future pregnancy by sprints, long jumps and somersaults (forwards and backwards), despite Göbbels complaining that girls should be graceful and good-looking and objecting reasonably: 'Why should a future mother go route-marching with a pack on her back?' The nation's fathers were meanwhile dressed like Boy Scouts in lederhosen in the Hitler Youth, which vigorously, if prematurely, practised what Hitler preached sexually after its evening parades.

Kinder, Kirche, Küche remained officially the woman's lot. Married women doctors had been fired by Hitler immediately on his taking power, and women banned from juries because 'they cannot think logically or reason objectively, since they are ruled only by emotion'. They were not to wear fashionable clothes, though fancy-dress regional costumes were encouraged, and they were not to smoke in the street. A growing girl's duty to breed was complicated by unemployment and the second duty of joyful work, organised by the Reich Labour Service for Young Women. The compulsory Domestic Service year – being an *au pair* in your own country – failed, because mothers put their daughters out to their neighbours, just to do the washing-up. Some became Land Girls, some advanced at seventeen into the Faith and Beauty Scheme, which more promisingly involved learning elegantly to dance, play tennis and sunbathe.

Though three million German women did war work in 1918, Hitler remained intolerant of them working in munitions factories (in 1941 Churchill conscripted British women). Wartime Germany quickly discovered that it could not do without them. A year's labour service became compulsory for women under twenty-five, and after Stalingrad in 1943 all German women, between seventeen and forty-five were conscripted. Though fewer than a million ended as workers – *Schlesische Tageszeitung* – 'factory fear' was rife, despite their jobs being so glamorised in photographs from the German Labour Front that even the tram-cleaners looked joyous.

Many Germans, male and female, were unfortunately as short and dark as Hitler. So breeders of the master race needed to spring from the racially élite SS, to pair with the blonde, blue-eyed graduates of the Women's Academy of Wisdom and Culture (that was Himmler's idea, anyway). Their children should preferably be boys, which could be achieved by the couple giving up drink for a week, then the man walking 20 kilometres and waking up his wife for copulation on his return (another of Himmler's ideas). The *Lebensborn*, the SS Fount of Life Club (motto: Every mother of good blood is our sacred trust), provided splendid obstetric hospitals for the SS men's mates (they had a 6:4 ratio of wed to unwed), if 'racially and genetically valuable'.

The SS responded ungratefully, the officers managing only 1.41 children each and a miserable 1.1 coming from the ranks. Porridge was served in these hospitals for breakfast because of its healthy slimming effect, as displayed by the English aristocrats, who ate it every morning (Himmler said so). Himmler wanted all women of thirty with no children to be allowed – later to be forced – into the hospitals through previous use of his selected 'reproduction assistants', but this idea was overtaken by events. So was Hitler's, of awarding Germany's bravest medal winners with legalised bigamy.

The absence of marriage was declared irrelevant to the veneration of motherhood, and the other inescapable irregularities of sex were disposed of in a similar forthright way. 'Homosexual behaviour, in particular, merits no mercy,' judged the Reich legal chief Hans Frank (hanged at Nürnberg, wearing a Cheviot tweed suit). The foul fault of male homosexuality was its not producing babies for Hitler, though lesbianism was passable because an insistent man might get round it. Pudgy Ernst Röhm and his handsome friends who ran the SA Brownshirts were wildly homosexual, but Hitler prevented this being any embarrassment to the Nazi hierarchy by shooting the lot on the Night of the Long Knives. Revival was mooted of the medicval practice of drowning homosexuals in a bog, but Himmler jokingly conceded the shortage of bogs, adding that homosexual SS men (about one discovered a month) must 'on my instructions, be taken to a concentration camp and there shot while attempting to escape'.

Child abusers were castrated: 238 in 1939. Sex murderers were executed – the man who committed fifty-four of them by 1943 was desired by Göbbels to be burnt alive and quartered. But it was an intriguing oddity of Hitler's often to reprieve them.

The horror of German girls copulating with Polish and other prisoners was resolved by the Gestapo hanging the men from trees and having their fellows file past them. Almost 10,000 German women were prosecuted for sex with foreign workers during 1942, when this moral danger was humanely diverted by the establishment of brothels with 600 prostitutes imported from Paris (they did well, returning home to buy apartment blocks). The German Army in 1939 enjoyed medically supervised prostitution, as the British Army had in 1864. These military brothels had an additional usc in the research to substitute semen for plasma in blood transfusions, the condoms being carefully collected by the girls after use and gathered regularly by the researchers.

Hitler had a quirk about syphilis. He explained with sweeping outrage its ultimate cause (apart from the Jews) in *Mein Kampf*:

Theatre, art, literature, cinema, press, posters, and window displays must be cleansed of all manifestations of our rotting world and placed in the service of a moral, political, and cultural idea. Public life must be freed from the stifling perfume of our modern eroticism, just as it must be freed from all unmanly, prudish hypocrisy. [No disagreement from our own self-important moralists.]

Only after these measures are carried out can the medical struggle against the plague itself be carried through with any prospect of success. But here, too, there must be no half-measures; the gravest and most ruthless decisions will have to be made. It is a half-measure to let incurably sick people steadily contaminate the remaining healthy ones. This is in keeping with the humanitarianism which, to avoid hurting one individual, lets a hundred others perish. The demand that defective people be prevented from propagating equally defective offspring is a demand of the clearest reason and if systematically executed represents the most humane act of mankind.

The insane garrulity presents an approach, and an excuse, which he applied more generally and murderously across Europe.

Hitler's antagonism to the syphilitic spirochaete has aroused suspicion that he himself suffered from it, and that the world suffered from its mental effects. But the Russians found no trace of syphilis in his admittedly partly burnt body; more decisively, all Hitler's writings about the disease indicate that he really knew nothing about it.

The commonest sexual temptation is interfering in the sex lives of others. The worthy West German Morality League, founded in 1885, stoutly supported everything sexual which Hitler suggested, from his immediate banning of nudism in 1933 as a sexual aberration. Let today's religious, moral, or busy bodies recall the company they keep. And that even the Nazis failed to stop humans copulating with those they should not, or to make them copulate with those that they should. Hitler's mystical plan after 1933 to proliferate a warlike German master race had a negligible impact on history, compared with the mundane proliferation after 1942 of American aircraft and armaments, which blew such ideas to bits.

ELEVEN

Sexual Oddities

....

All the world is queer save thee and me, and even thou art
a little queer.

Robert Owen, 1828

....

Oddballs

On 30 April 1993, between sets at Hamburg, the previous
year's Wimbledon lady finalist, nineteen-year-old
Monica Seles of Yugoslavia, was stabbed from behind
with a long-bladed sharp-pointed knife by a male spectator. He had no trouble reaching over the three-foot
barrier as she sat towelling herself by the umpire's chair:
she screamed, ran into centre court and collapsed. Her
thirty-eight-year-old assailant, observed as 'weird-look-
ing', was bundled away by four guards and the next day
pronounced mentally ill. He had struck at Monica
through devotion to her Wimbledon Centre Court victor,
twenty-three-year-old Steffi Graf of Germany. He wished
to spare his beloved Steffi from Monica's rising rivalry
(young Monica had already made £4.5 million in prize
money). Monica luckily suffered no worse than a cut an
inch deep, but it kept her out of tennis, and at the French
Open Championship in May one of her own male devo-

tees shouted angrily at Steffi that the attack was all her fault.

Such unwelcome love from a stranger had the previous year been suffered in London by the Duke of Kent's daughter, twenty-nine-year-old Lady Helen Windsor. A freelance cameraman aged thirty-six had faced the charge of her assault, which was dropped on his admission to a mental hospital. An occupational hazard of popular actresses is similarly an alarmingly fierce sexual adherence, developing in one of their otherwise innocuously worshipful fans. Doctors, vicars and celibate priests spasmodically discover themselves passionately adored by women they can barely remember, or even recognise in the street. That the romantic object is not usually aware that any affection exists, or even that the lover himself or herself exists, makes so powerful an attachment all the odder. The only passionate feeling of the loved one is to keep as far away from the wooer as possible.

All was explained in 1942 by the psychiatrist C. G. de Clérambault in Paris. His book, *Les Psychoses Passionelles*, christened with his own name this syndrome of fervent amorous delusion, which has been observed to flit through human minds since those which were attended by Hippocrates.

Men have imagined themselves betrothed to goddesses, women have been convinced they were panted after by kings. Boccaccio spins the tale of Lisa, the prosperous apothecary's daughter of Salerno. She 'grew fervently enamoured' of King Pedro of Arragon, whom she had but glimpsed through her window jousting. So despairing a passion reduced her to sickness and distaste for life. The King heard about it over breakfast from an itinerant musician, and being the decent sort shortly arrived in state at the apothecary's garden, where he selected from his entourage a young man 'of gentle birth, but poor circumstances', presented him to Lisa as her husband, gave her a kiss and cured her.

The most starry-eyed of de Clérambault's cases was a French dressmaker in her fifties who had caused the stout and bearded King of England, George V, to fall desperately in love with her. During the Great War, the British uniforms she encountered in France all adorned messengers who she instinctively knew were expressing his passion. After the Armistice, she became a regular tourist outside the railings of Buckingham Palace, waiting for His Majesty to emerge and carry her off. She had sadly to satisfy herself with his signalling to her across the ceremonially guarded forecourt by drawing the curtains of the palace windows. Later, the King rounded on her, and in London stole her luggage, which was stuffed with his pictures. But she forgave him, though she suffered heartbreakingly for having offended him with her tenderness. She had earlier enjoyed the love of his father, Edward VII, but, unlike the actress Lillie Langtry and many other ladies, only in the imagination.

The typical sufferer from de Clérambault's syndrome is a youngish woman who precipitously discovers a male social or managerial superior to be violently in love with her. His passion is expressed by a casual meeting, by a subtle glance, by a coded remark – to her excitement, it is confirmed by regular, if almost undetectable, similar signs of camouflaged passion. Everybody of course knows about the affair, and impart their knowledge of it to her with equally careful hints and masked gestures. She writes to him, telephones, lies in wait. His wife is an irrelevance, any interference from her in the throbbing romance to be brushed aside by physical attack. Perhaps the man genuinely responds to her first advances, is interested, flattered, aroused; but with their persistence he turns alarmed and desperate, seeking refuge in the courts with injunctions and prosecutions. The woman's passion can persist through years of separation, and its final undeniable rejection leads to her despair and suicide.

Such near imperceptible intimations can contrarily inspire the fierce jealousy of the Othello syndrome. Within the mind of its sufferers, the green-eyed monster which ate Desdemona is easily aroused – by misconstrued chat at a party, or by some intensely inspected stains on a skirt, or by some fancied changes in a wife's attitude or innocent ones in her everyday movements. (The French husband in the *fin de siècle* cartoon, helpfully undoing, from behind, the top of his pretty wife's stays at bedtime with the remark: 'Ah! This morning I made a knot on this lacing, and tonight there's a bow,' had a more realistic justification.)

The imagined extramarital lover is identified and confronted, is mystified, is perhaps assaulted. A wife might interpret her husband's normally appreciative eye for sexy women on television, in magazines, or in the flesh, as proof of his widely roving affections, and fall upon him with a kitchen knife. Or an unresponsive wife may suffer from a weak sexual drive, which is construed by her husband as sexual exhaustion incurred from the neighbours. Or such jealousy in either husband or wife may simply be the disjointed expression of their secreted infidelity or homosexuality.

These two syndromes incorporate the psychological abnormalities of delusion, obsession and imagined persecution, concentrated in a sexual beam upon a single person.

That men and women could be insane with love is of ancient speculation.

Sir Alexander Crichton of the Westminster Hospital was a surgeon who so hated operating on the eighteenth-century's unanaesthetised patients that he became professionally reborn as a painless physician. Later, he was made doctor to Tsar Alexander I and ran the Russian health service. Sir Alexander was the first to suggest, in his *Mental Derangement* of 1798, that people who fancied themselves to be violently in love with someone, but whose target was indifferent to, or ignorant of, the compliment, were presenting a frank symptom of madness. In 1848, Sir Alexander Morrison from Edinburgh, who combined being inspector of the lunatic asylums of Surrey with physician to Queen Charlotte, in his *Lectures on the Nature, Causes and Treatment of Insanity* coined 'erotomania' for a delusive amorous insanity, directed upon a single subject. He differentiated it from the poetic sighs and tears of 'love melancholy', which he considered normal.

A forensic medicine textbook elaborated on his definition in 1887: 'Extreme sexual passion is called erotomania in both sexes'. The *Lexicon of Medicine* had earlier cautiously mentioned that: 'By some authors the term is restricted to those cases in which the imagination alone is affected; by others the grosser forms nymphomania and satyriasis are included'.

A decorous line needs to be drawn, between the romping nymphs and satyrs who display a stark enthusiasm for sexual intercourse and severe sufferers from the acute symptoms of everyday love. But the uncritical affection of 'normal' love, the admiration and attentiveness directed intensely upon a solitary person – even one who accepts and returns it with equal enthusiasm and bliss – the incessant lodgement of the lover in the other lover's mind, all compose an attitude which is delightful and artistically highly inspirational, but plainly mildly barmy. We are all madly in love. The biological urge to reproduce, refined even to exquisite delicacy in the highest human minds, is none the less an abnormal psychological state which can worsen suddenly into familiar catastrophes. Love can bring cruelty and treachery, dishonesty and deceit, resentment and revenge, melancholy and suicide, hate and murder.

Furor amoris, Cicero decided. How odd, that love should be the most violent of our emotions.

Sharing the Labour

'Couvade' is derived from the French 'to hatch'. *Faire la couvade* was being contemptuously applied in 1611 to campaigners who preferred 'to sit cowring or skowking within dores, to lurke in the campe when Gallants are at the Battel'. It now describes the signs of pregnancy and labour occurring in the father as well as the mother.

The obstetrical oddity started as a ritual. The father took to his bed synchronously with the mother; he fasted, groaned and was tenderly attended by women as though himself about to give birth. The rite was noticed in Rhodes in 250 BC; in Corsica by Julius Caesar's contemporary Diodorus; in the first century it was observed by Strabo the Stoic traveller; Marco Polo saw it in the thirteenth in the Chinese province of West Yunnan; meanwhile the Basques, the Indians, the Siamese, the Russians and the native Americans were all doing it.

The ceremony may have been to emphasise the fatherhood of the child, of which the motherhood was being so emphatically demonstrated. Or it may have been an act of magic, the father deceiving the malicious but gullible spirits, alarmingly set to torture and perhaps to kill the mother, to project their evils innocuously upon himself. Marco Polo thought it anyway only fair that the husband should suffer some of the exceptional toil and trouble of childbirth.

What began as a performance became a malady. One

in ten fathers today suffers some mentally inspired symptoms during the pregnancy.

In the first trimester of his partner's pregnancy, the father, too, has early-morning nausea and vomiting, and vague abdominal pains. As an assertion that his sufferings are more than mimicry, he sometimes starts undergoing them before she even knows that she is pregnant. Sometimes he has cravings for items like strawberries in January, or for papaws, or *pâté de foie gras* or chocolates, which match the mother's simultaneous longings for entirely different *bonnes bouches*. As her labour approaches, the father develops acute abdominal pain, which may land him as well in hospital, for an emergency appendicectomy. During the pregnancy, the father's abdomen, too, may have swollen. This is accomplished by the combination of an arched spine and a depressed diaphragm, the mechanism which produces in the female the psychological disorder of pseudocyesis, a false pregnancy. One husband suffered couvade while his wife was suffering only this.

Couvade is common among men on active service who have left a pregnant partner at home: they suffer abdominal pains, which exacerbate when they know that labour is due, and cease on news of a successful delivery. Toothache, a Shakespearian sign of love, was also a painful expression of couvade, which caused Elizabethan married men with bad teeth to get their legs pulled about incipient fatherhood. Francis Bacon recorded the couvade in those witch-hunting days when it could be construed as a spell, and many odd old women were seized, accused, tortured, tried and burnt for casting it. An unsuccessful intrusion of feminism into the couvade occurred in Edinburgh Castle on 19 June 1566, when Mary Queen of Scots went into labour with the future James VI, and a lady-in-waiting transferred her pains to the willing and honoured Lady Reres, who writhed dutifully on her bed. But so did the Queen.

The sickness and pains of couvade may be a roundabout expression of the guilt felt by the father for endangering his wife by making her pregnant. It should have become a rare disease in the past thirty years, when fathers have been welcomed in the delivery room of the hospital labour suite to watch the birth. The only case I heard of an agonised father during delivery occurred when the mother's bed needed urgently to be moved through failure of the main light, and the agitated father began howling pitifully. 'If you can't shut up, get out,' ordered the exasperated midwife. 'I'd like to,' he replied enthusiastically, 'if only you'd get the end of this bloody bed off my foot.'

Unkind Cuts

The penis is a marvel of hydraulic engineering. In its enduring, reliable and repetitive efficiency it may be compared to the Gatun locks of the Panama Canal, which since 1914 have been raising ocean liners with swift and safe smoothness to 85 feet above the Atlantic and Pacific swell. The unstoppable power of the penile mechanism matches in ingenuity the channelling of mountain torrents, which since 1910 have whirred the turbines brilliantly to electrify the lamps of innumerable distant towns. The clever simplicity of penile erection, in applying fluid pressure to achieve motive power, recalls the mechanics of the hydraulic ram, or of the water-mills once scattered across the land, which ground away steadily and were esteemed both aesthetically and functionally by everyone.

In the anatomical eye of Gray:

The penis is a pendulous organ suspended from the front and sides of the pubic arch and containing the greater part of the urethra. In the flaccid condition it is cylindrical in shape, but when erect it assumes the form of a triangular prism with rounded angles, one side of the prism forming the dorsum of the penis.

The penis is a marvellously expandable one-shot weapon. It is composed mostly of spongy tissue, the *corpora cavernosa penis*. The organ itself is firmly based through two diverging *crura* of this cavernous body, attached behind to the bottom of the pubic bones. These are the bones which join low in the mid-line of the abdomen at the pubic synthesis, to complete the pelvic basin into which our digestive organs are heaped.

'Its anterior end suddenly expands to form an obtuse cone, named the *glans penis*,' says Gray, seemingly surprised. He adds with anatomists' meticulousness: 'The projecting margin of its base is named the *corona glandis*, and the constriction behind the latter is known as the *neck of the penis*.' He notices that the corona and the neck have 'numerous small *preputial glands*; these secrete a sebaceous material named *smegma*, which possesses a very peculiar odour.'

The *corpus spongiosum penis* is a second porous strip, which is clasped above by the *corpora cavernosa penis*. The *corpus spongiosum* is the lagging round the penile piping: the *urethra*, which runs from the bladder to the porcelain of the outside world. With Nature's recurrent economy, this provides an exit for both urine and sperm.

The penis is nourished with blood both by its deep arteries and by twin arteries which run along the *dorsum*. As the *dorsum* anatomically defines the back of the penis, which usually hangs down facing frontwards and joins the dorsal planes of the body only on erection, this excited state seems to be taken genially by Gray and his colleagues as its normal one.

The dorsal nerves of the penis, which run with the arteries like electrical cables with the household water mains, spring from the pudendal nerve ('the nerve of shame'), which arises from the complex sacral plexus extruded by the spinal cord at the back of the pelvis, which gives also the sciatic nerve running down the leg.

The filamentous branches of these dorsal nerves have 'peculiar end-bulbs' to innervate the skin sheathing the penis, which, observes Gray, 'is remarkable for its thinness, its dark colour, its looseness of connexion with the fibrous envelope of the organ, and the absence of adipose tissue'. Stimulation of these nerves – indeed, anticipation of their stimulation, even remote, even imaginary – reflexly relaxes the penile arteries, flooding the empty caverns with blood and instantly creating a rigid organ, bursting to function, which has swivelled 180 degrees upwards through the air.

The penis's defiance of the law of gravity is a singularity which is barely noticed by its possessors, or its recipients, at the time. The phenomenon made a lasting impression on Sigmund Freud, who in 1899 reasoned that his Viennese female patients' dreams of flying – so frequent, and so delightful – must needs be interpreted as longings for sexual excitement. Earlier patients expressed these night-time desires through the balloons which had been gently rising over Europe throughout the century, since the pioneering aeronautical Montgolfiers of France; but Count Zeppelin, by the outbreak of the Great War, had provided a more fitting shape to arise over dreamland.

The penis presents a foreskin which overlaps the thrustful, rounded fore-end of the glans. This *prepuce* – in Latin *praeputium*, coined by the first-century satirist Juvenal – is a removable collar of functionless tissue which throughout history has maintained a wildly exaggerated importance.

This is on two counts:

1 *Medical*

Phimosis – Greek for muzzling – means a foreskin so tight-fitting that it cannot be slipped backwards over the smooth skin of the glans. At birth this is common; by the age of five unusual. The delicate fibres connecting the two surfaces are absorbed during infancy, and by burgeoning puberty only one per cent of lads cannot flip their foreskins back.

Balanitis is infection of the potential space between glans and foreskin. It can be caused by the excessive formation of the *smegma* which smelt so peculiar to Gray; by sand in children dwelling in deserts; by burning, through ammoniacal urine neglected on wet nappies; or by dirty habits. 'Surgeons and urologists in Britain know that many men conceal a dirty mess beneath the foreskin,' the *British Medical Journal* was once sniffing. The *BMJ* advised that 'Examination of the penis, as well as the testes, should be a standard part of school medical inspections'. Which, it added severely, if hopefully, 'would provide an excellent opportunity to back up or amplify parental instruction in personal hygiene'.

Paraphimosis is swelling of the glans when the foreskin has slipped back after penile use and has not been replaced, and so acts as a tourniquet.

None of these conditions is a provocation for circumcising newborn infants. An infected, mucky, penile far end is easily curable with the creams used for nappy rash (which is what it is). Nor is circumcision of use to prevent the development of a narrow urinary nozzle ('pinhole meatus') causing difficulty in peeing. Nor did it back up the Victorians' enthusiasm for preventing masturbation (with which their pedagogues were unhealthily obsessed). Nor did it diminish Victorian sexual delight (and thus make copulation so joyless that it was hardly worthwhile being immoral). Nor does circumcision forestall cancer of the penis, which is found only after a long lifetime of use; nor does circumcision prevent cancer of the wife's cervix. Nor does it elevate the psychological state of the father, who is ordering the operation as a substitution for castrating his son, to express his authority in the home (well, Freud thought so).

The operation of infant circumcision is simple. The foreskin is easily removed with a snip down the back and then a few round the base, like skinning a green fig. It has its dangers. The entire skin of the shaft of the penis may be ineptly removed, leaving the poor little organ raw. The glans may be clumsily nicked, and there are antibiotic-resistant germs prowling every hospital to pounce and chew it to bits. Using the electric cautery instead of scissors to cut off the foreskin is simpler, but it has the danger of sizzling the infantile penis to a cinder. And it is coming to be recognised that newborn infants complain of operative and postoperative pain as keenly as their parents, but nobody takes any notice of the pathetic things.

2 *Ritual*

Newborn infants are circumcised by Jews and Muslims, because they like it that way. The aborigines knocked out a boy's tooth as a preliminary, and in New Guinea the rite was performed in a long hut shaped like a monster with goggle eyes and gaping mouth, to the powerful music of bull-roarers – short strips of wood (preferably from trees struck by lightning) whirled on a cord round the head. Nineteenth-century Christians regarded circumcision with horror, but some Empire builders had it done to facilitate the seduction of Muslim-women.

As the century turned, circumcision came into vogue

with the British upper and proliferating middle classes, under the stimulus of doctors. Some practitioners were so convinced of the operation's hygienic worthiness that they touted from the birth notices in the newspapers, suggesting that the boy's father, too, might care to enjoy its belated benefits. By the 1930s, most public schoolboys had been circumcised as unquestioningly as they were later to be confirmed by a bishop. Army officers were thus generally circumcised, if the ranks presented only the one per cent rate suffered by the working class. During World War Two, in a POW camp in Germany one officer was singled out for harsh treatment, causing a delegation of his comrades to ask why. The Nazi commandant explained that the man was a Jew. He was circumcised. The officers looked at each other, unbuttoned their khaki flies, and waggled their circumcised willies at the commandant. The day was saved. Circumcision in Britain commendably declined when the National Health Service decreed that the parents had to pay for it. In the United States, the parents of the two million boys born there every year also have to pay for it, and the doctors make sure that 80 per cent of them cheerfully do, making the profession a handy few million dollars a year.

The Enigma of Female Circumcision

What?

Anatomy may be boring, but it is, thankfully, unemotional. Let us again consult Mr Henry Gray, FRS, FRCS, lecturer at St George's Hospital, London, in 1861:

> The *external genital organs of the female*
> (pudendum muliebre) are: the mons pubis, the

labia majora et minora pudendi, the clitoris, the vestibule of the vagina . . .

The *mons pubis*, the rounded eminence in front of the pubic symphysis, is formed by a collection of fatty tissue beneath the skin. It becomes covered with hair at the time of puberty over an area which has a horizontal upper limit, whereas in the male the pubic hair extends upwards towards the umbilicus in and near the median plane.

The *labia majora* are two prominent, longitudinal, cutaneous folds which extend downwards and backwards from the mons pubis, and form the lateral boundaries of a fissure or cleft, named the *pudendal cleft*, into which the vagina and urethra open.

The *labia minora* are two small cutaneous folds, situated between the labia majora, and extending from the clitoris obliquely downwards, laterally and backwards for about 4 cm on each side of the orifice of the vagina . . .

The *clitoris* is an erectile structure, homologous with the penis.

The *hymen vaginæ* is a thin fold of mucous membrane situated at the orifice of the vagina . . .

Female circumcision has three versions:

1 Removal of the tiny prepuce of the clitoris, the counterpart of male circumcision.

2 Removal of the clitoris and a token part, or all, of the labia minora.

3 A single cut removing completely the clitoris, labia minora and labia majora. This is the counterpart of 'infibulation', the fastening to the prepuce of a fibula or buckle, 'an operation performed on young boys and singers by the Romans, who used it as a muzzle to human incontinence'. It was brought to the notice of the English by the sermons of John Wesley. Infib-

ulation can be achieved less traumatically by sewing up the female's pudendal cleft.

Where?

Strabo from Greece observed in the first century female circumcision, as well as the couvade. His seventeen-volume *Geographica* records it in Egypt, together with the way they fed the sacred crocodiles. Old Harrovian James Bruce saw it in 1770, when exploring the sources of the Blue Nile in Ethiopia. The scholarly explorer Sir Richard Burton – expert on Mohammedans, he made the pilgrimage to Mecca in disguise (as 'Al-Haj Abdulla') – in 1856 added to his *First Footsteps in East Africa* 'A Brief Description of Certain Peculiar Customs'. This recorded the full female circumcision then being performed in Somalia and Ethiopia. Even written in Latin, it terrified his publisher, who cut it out, but – as occurs among publishers – someone printed it by mistake. The operation is still performed in the countries across mid-Africa, including Senegal, Mali, Sudan, Zaïre and Kenya, and 75 million living women have had it. In the 1860s, clitorectomy was introduced into Britain and the United States by Dr Baker Brown, as treatment for masturbation, nymphomania, hysteria and bounding feminism, but the idea did not catch on.

How?

The operation of female circumcision was described and photographed shortly after World War Two by a London professor of tropical hygiene. It occurred among the M'Bwake tribe living in the remote forests of north Zaïre against the Ubangi river, which forms the frontier with the ex-French Central African Republic. The patients, aged between ten and fourteen, were painted with white zigzags across their bare bodies and white dots outlining their faces and running down their noses; their necks were ringed with rows of beads and they wore close-fitting hats of bright cloth.

The operating team moved into a secluded part of the forest. Everyone is singing and dancing. A young man lies on his back, knees bent, feet astride. His thighs, covered with leaves, make the operating table. The naked girl is laid on her back, her head on his belly; he grasps her wrists, the elderly (and well-paid) female operator parts her legs, pulls forward her clitoris towards the mons pubis, and with a sliver of glass excises clitoris and both labia minora and majora at a stroke. There is no analgesia. If the girl struggles, she gets a cut anus and rectum.

The child is sat on the ground, her back against a tree. The profusely bleeding ragged wound between her thighs is dressed with some white chicken feathers. Her legs are tied together and she is carried to an isolated hut, in the care of another old woman for a month to get over it. Immediate after-effects are haemorrhage, infection (including tetanus) and urinary retention; later, painful copulation, infertility, heavy menstrual bleeding and pain, and pelvic sepsis. The wound heals with inelastic fibrous tissue, a matchstick holding open the vagina. After the inevitable tearing of childbirth later, it mends all the tougher.

Why?

To make the woman less sexy, and thus her future husband's mind easier: a girl might not find a husband without it. (Though some husbands think it makes their wives sexier.) Circumcision expresses the girl's sexual maturity: she becomes abruptly an adult, a full member of the tribe. The clitoris is an aggressive male intrusion, incongruous on a girl, as the foreskin is a feminine one misplaced on a boy. The operation is for both sexes a cleansing, a beautification.

Wherefore?

Female circumcision was condemned by the missionaries – particularly by the medical missionaries – all this century. Their campaign had the sadly predictable effect of anyone trying to stop anyone doing ill to themselves – drinking, smoking, drug-taking, jumping off Beachy Head. This was exemplified by its history in Kenya.

In 1929, the Protestant missionaries to the Kikuyu tribe, who are one and a half million Bantu-speaking peasant farmers living in the forests south of Mount Kenya around Nairobi, expelled from the church all apologists for female circumcision. Inevitably, an opposing organisation was founded, the Kikuyu Central Association of 1920, which accused the missionaries of threatening tribal unity. The British Government, running Kenya, took the British view of regret but inaction.

The Association's secretary was nationalist Jomo Kenyatta, later the power behind the revolutionary terrorists Mau Mau, who trod the familiar trail of imprisonment by the British to becoming President of his newly liberated country.

In 1935, Jomo Kenyatta was a student of anthropology at the London School of Economics. He read a paper on *irua* – female circumcision – which was to him little more than a nick in the loins to dampen a girl's sexual appetite, which had been seized upon by the colonists to shatter the Kikuyu's social structure. The seminar ended with Kenyatta and a British anthropologist shouting at each other across the lecture-room, a fierce controversy which would have baffled the assembly even had it not been conducted in Kikuyu.

'The real argument', Kenyatta insisted more coolly three years later, 'lies not in the defence of the surgical operation or its details but in the understanding of a very important fact in the tribal psychology of the Kikuyu – namely that this operation is still regarded as the very essence of an institution which has enormous educational, social, moral and religious implications ... The abolition of *irua* will destroy the tribal symbol which identifies the age-group and prevent the Kikuyu from perpetuating that spirit of collectivism and national solidarity which they have been able to maintain from time immemorial.'

This opportunist plea cut no ice at London dinnertables. The Duchess of Atholl pushed the Government to do something, but did not engineer the reprieve of a single Kenyan clitoris. Lord Kennet followed her in 1983, with a Bill in the House of Lords to outlaw the 'horrific' operation in Britain. Female circumcision was finally banned in Kenya by President Arap Moi in 1982, under the stimulation of fourteen children dying of it. It had been banned in Sudan in 1944, but continued clandestinely. It will in Kenya.

As Nairobi is only nine hours away from London, the operation is spasmodically performed privately in the Harley Street area. Like abortions in Britain before 1967, what is illegal or unprofessional for the doctor to perform competently is done in the back streets disastrously. In Paris in 1982, a baby from Mali bled to death after a Mali woman who had flown in with her removed her clitoris. The British Medical Association and the World Health Organisation continue to condemn the operation, to be countered by arguments about Western arrogance and traditional values and women's rights.

The argument for male or female circumcision are irrelevant. Our most powerful instinct is our reproductive one. Its organs incite in us such love and such terror, that we cannot prevent ourselves excitingly mucking about with them.

Dryden matches Robert Owen:

> There is a pleasure sure,
> In being mad, which none but madmen know!

And remember:

> There's a divinity which shapes our ends,
> Rough-hew them how we will.

TWELVE

The Sexual Scientific Revolution

. . . .

... the average American male has a penile length of 6.3 inches on erection.

Alfred C. Kinsey

... we find that the average (median) female in the sample had reached orgasm in something between 70 and 77 per cent of her marital coitus.

Alfred C. Kinsey et al

. . . .

More Useful Sexual Information

The length of time over which erection can be maintained during continuous erotic arousal, and before there is ejaculation, drops from an average of nearly an hour in the late teens and early twenties to 7 minutes in the 66–70 year old group.

Alfred C. Kinsey et al. *Sexual Behavior in the Human Male,* 1948

In any age group there is considerable variation in the angle at which the erect penis is carried on the standing male. The average position, calculated from all ages, is very slightly above the horizontal, but there are approximately 15 to 20 per cent of the cases where the angle is about 45° above the horizontal, and 8 to 10 per cent of males who carry the erect penis nearly vertically, more or less tightly against the belly.

Alfred C. Kinsey et al. *Sexual Behavior in the Human Female,* 1953

199

FREQUENCY OF ORGASM DURING
CLITORAL STIMULATION BY HAND

	Q.I	Q.II	Q.III		TOTAL
'Yes'	279	220	67	=	566
Always	16	36	25	=	77
Usually	9	102	24	=	135
Sometimes	12	40	17	=	69
Rarely	0	14	2	=	16
Total	316	412	135		863
Orgasm Regularity	44%	39%	49%	=	44%

Shere Hite, The Hite Report, 1976

Here is the rank order of the USA and four
international samples on the percentage of
students reporting they had engaged in coitus at
some time:

Males *Per cent having coitus*

1 The English university — 75
2 The Norwegian university — 67
3 The US student sample — 58
4 The Canadian university — 57
5 The German university — 55

Females

1 The English university — 63
2 The German university — 60
3 The Norwegian university — 54
4 The US student sample — 43
5 The Canadian university — 35

As indicated, we were able to obtain a sample of
only 48 Italian female students, and of those, 40
supplied information regarding sexual behaviour.
Obviously such a small sample can at best only
roughly suggest a situation at one particular
university in Italy. We indicate their responses
only because they are so dramatically different.

Vance Packard, The Sexual Wilderness, 1968

In the most extreme types of sexual reaction, an individual who has experienced orgasm may double and throw his whole body into continuous and violent motion, arch his back, throw his hips, twist his head, thrust out his arms and legs, verbalize, moan, groan, or scream in much the same way as a person who is suffering the extremes of torture. In all of these respects, human females and males react in essentially the same way. In some individuals the whole body may be thrown, or tossed, or rolled over a distance of several feet or yards. On occasion the sexual partner may be crushed, pounded, violently punched, or kicked during the uncontrolled responses of an intensely reactive individual.

Ruth and Edward Brecher (editors), *An Analysis of Human Sexual Response*, 1966

Damp Beds – Place a mirror between the sheets, where it should remain for a few minutes. If, when removed, the glass is misty the bed is damp.

Mrs Beeton's Household Management, c. 1955

Sex Education

Compulsory education was inflicted on England in 1880. State schools had already been provided by the Elementary Education Act of 1870, an item of offhand legislation by Mr Gladstone, who was preoccupied with Ireland, which as usual was experiencing troubles. Gladstone's enthusiasm for education was anyway restricted to its possible effect on religion. The Church of England already ran schools, both Sunday and weekday, which happily found their State grants suddenly doubled. But the Radical Nonconformists were furious at the notion of paying, through the rates, any school whether Church or State which provided religious instruction they did not agree with. The Conservatives helped the Liberal Government carry the Bill through Parliament, and the Radicals helped the Conservatives defeat Gladstone at the next election in 1874. The nation's education became a political dog's bone seventy years before the nation's health did, much more painfully.

'An education, when all written out on foolscap, covers nearly ten sheets,' perceived the most distinguished of the Professors of Economics at McGill University, in 1910. He added about its fate: 'Like the rest of us he is, or was until he forgot it all, an extremely well-educated man.' We can all recall vividly delights and humiliations from our schooldays, but of the schooling itself we can reach for little more than is necessary to finish, sometimes, the crossword in the morning paper. We certainly could not refill Stephen Leacock's ten foolscap sheets with the information which we spent a dozen immature and highly distractible years assimilating. Luckily, the cascade of scientific invention in the second half of this century has made education inessential.

There is no longer the necessity to learn to read, because television comfortably transforms for us everything readable, from the day's news to the eternal classics; while symbols as explicit as Chinese characters flourish everywhere to indicate important particularisations like 'Gents', 'Roadworks', 'No Smoking', 'No Dogs' and '!'. Mathematics is redundant, with the bar code to tot up our bill and the miniature calculator to check it. Who needs to learn to write, with a telephone in every pocket and handbag? Geography is superfluous, now airlines so cheaply and so swiftly take us everywhere to see for ourselves. History but clutters the mind, in a world changing with a breathtaking suddenness which is interpreted incessantly by impressively skilled radio and TV commentators. Why learn languages, when the pressing integration of the world's nations means that everyone must grudgingly learn to speak English? For religious education, we can bring beatific smiles to the ecclesiastical establishment every Sunday by going to church.

Education should be sought as a privilege by academic enthusiasts, as sports facilities by keen athletes. Before 1870, the school-leavers were aged eleven, and two million children did not go to school at all. Doubling this figure to match population growth, that number of truants would not in the slightest incommode civilisation today. Better, they would patriotically save money.

One and a half million British students now swat at our higher educational establishments, at the cost of £7 billion a year. Expenditure on all education by central and local government is £27 billion a year. Allowing higher education to continue flourishing, and allowing another £5 billion a year for schooling the inexpensively apt applicants for it, this would free £15 billion to help out the National Health Service's annual costs of £30.5 billion. The transfer would forestall a savage rationing of treatment, which is becoming inevitable with a population disinclined to pay more for anything so unpleasant as sickness and disability, served by politicians terrified to offend them by raising taxes. Education should instruct only the clever, as the NHS treats only the ill. It is better to be alive and illiterate than well educated and dead.

Clearly a decision so serious as whether or not voluntarily to submit to education cannot be made by the unripe mind. This peril can be avoided by raising the school-entering age to sixteen. Two years from sixteen to eighteen is adequate for the maturer brain to absorb a classroom education from scratch.

The first, if unmentioned, duty of education is relieving parents of their trying children during most of the day for most of the year. But mothers now go out to work as readily as fathers, happily leaving their younger children with minders. So they did before 1880, or more thriftily dosed them after breakfast with opium and left them at home. Soon the infants were sufficiently mobile to strengthen the family income, though after 1876 children were delayed by Parliament from starting work until aged ten. The cotton mills of Lancashire provided these little ones with appropriately unexacting employment, which today would be bettered by the thriving electronics industry. The physical work is light, and even the youngest children enjoy a brilliant aptitude for the subject. This is painfully clear to parents, who must resign to their children manipulation of even the simpler expressions of electronics in video recorders and computer games.

The ridiculous antithesis of superfluous scholarly education is sex education having become universal and compulsory.

In July 1983, Mr Major matched up to Mr Gladstone, though he was similarly preoccupied with Ireland, which was still having troubles. Amendment No. 62 to the Education Act obliged secondary schools to provide sex education, though the House of Lords added another amendment to allow children to play truant if their parents preferred to keep them in the dark. Both items of legislation were anyway unnecessary, because humans of all ages felt an overpowering obligation to know absolutely everything about sex, and were enthusiastically educating themselves.

Sex Higher Education

Around the turn of the eighteenth century, when Michael Faraday was organising electricity and Humphrey Davy was sorting out chemistry, the Revd

Thomas Malthus discouragingly indicated that the world was copulating itself to death. This was through the fruits thereof gobbling up the fruits of the earth and starving themselves. It was the first intrusion of budding science into primordial sex.

In 1876, the American Dr Charles Knowlton wrote *Fruits of Philosophy, or the Private Companion of Young Married People*, a reticent sex manual which advised on contraception. It was predictably received in Britain as 'a dirty, filthy book . . . no decently educated English husband would allow even his wife to have it', according to prosecuting counsel when its publishers, Charles Bradlaugh MP and Anne Besant, both got six months at the Old Bailey. The genteel *Married Love* by the unbearable, egoistic Marie Stopes PhD (Munich), the Joan of Arc of contraception, appeared in 1918, escaped prosecution and sold splendidly. It was congratulated by *The Practitioner* for offering doctors information about sex of which they were ignorant, and of which they might largely disapprove.

A Marie Stopes supporter observed in the *Guy's Hospital Gazette* in 1924: 'The language is in places flowery and highly-coloured, and of such a nature as to inflame the imagination of both young and old', adding flatteringly that her books were 'read extensively and secretly in girls' schools, where they are passed round, and by boys in the same spirit that indecent literature in general is enjoyed'. Also that they were read by flappers all over the country, though if read by girls of dubious virtue could be considered as practical handbooks of prostitution. The doctor blamed all this on the stuffy, sexually unenlightened medical profession.

Sex is now the most favoured branch of popular science, outshining interest in the mechanics of the internal combustion engine, or the performance of home fermentation of wines and beer. Sex bobs about upon the flood of scientific achievement swamping everyday life, and has become an object of intense study by experts.

At the end of World War Two, Alfred C. Kinsey's *Sexual Behavior in the Human Male* appeared from Philadelphia. This 800-page book with 173 figures and 162 tables soared from the Marie Stopes elementary schoolroom, by applying scientific scrutiny to sex as though it were some widespread disease. Its varied symptoms were examined impassionedly by this Professor of Zoology at Indiana University, leaving the whole world standing amazed at the statistical things it had been doing without noticing it.

How many single men aged fifteen to twenty knew that they shared with a sample of another 2,868 single men a mean frequency of 0.32 nocturnal emissions a week, which was 11.29 per cent of the total nocturnal emmisions outlet? What married men aged thirty-six to forty were aware that they shared with 390 comrades a 0.11 frequency of these unruly emissions, or 4.40 per cent of the whole outlet? Any man from adolescence to sixty could now determine instantly the status of his nocturnal emissions from fingering a page covered with 250 sets of figures.

From another conscientious table, a male adolescent who was struck by puberty at thirteen, but with an educational level of 9 to 12, could console himself that his weekly sexual outlet frequency of 3.63 compared favourably with the 2.56 of a similar lad with an educational level of 13 plus. But on reaching the age of thirty-five, 34.6 per cent of the cleverer ones will have intercourse with prostitutes, compared with a regrettable 72.7 per cent of the dimwits. Couples in their late twenties of the lower white-collar class copulate 2.33 times a week, but in the professional classes they do it 0.17 times a week more. Couples of similar ages in the 0 to 8 education scale have the wife on top 24.3 per cent of times, but in the 13–plus scale this almost doubles to 42.9 times (my remarks above about the present futility of education have a possible flaw). And 20 per cent of the rural population of the United States aged twenty-five do it with animals.

The newspapers and broadcasting of the world had just been pulverised by the supreme scientific achievement of the atom bomb, and applied to the Kinsey report a fitting reverence. Five years later, Kinsey did the same job for women. Statistics henceforth fashionably overlaid passion in the popular sex manuals, which became more satisfyingly titillating as the century advanced and prudery dropped below the pubis. Dr Alex Comfort's illustrated *The Joy of Sex* has plundered the bookshops since 1972, even if its pictured participants look as joyless as sitting at the dentist's. Instructors in sex became seized with a solemnity towards their subject approaching that of instructors in religion. The only cheerful sex guide was published by the British Health Education Authority in 1994, Nick Fisher's *Your Pocket Guide to Sex*, which was also practical, lucid, and short, and was instantly banned by the British Government and vilified by its Minister of Health as 'smutty'.

Sex guides have complemented in profitable proliferation slimming guides, each with as little beneficial effect on their optimistic readers. Nothing is necessary for slimming beyond eating less; and it is misleading to parade various raptures when the bodily apparatus for eliciting the sexual reflex is frugally limited. 'Your body has nine doors and I have opened them all,' wrote Guillaume Apollinaire in his *Poem to Louise de Coligny*, but he must have included her nostrils and armpits.

What Makes a Man and *What Makes a Woman Good in Bed* were shrewd titles of the 1980s, but more inviting for the reader than useful. We express but our characters in our sex responses, as in our social responses: the brash, the shy, the selfish, the vain, the cruel, and the tender and compassionate, are much the same when encountered in bed as on the bus. The pleasure of sex, like all pleasures, lies largely in our state of mind at the time.

God would be puzzled at such preoccupied elaboration of a simple, if strong, biological urge. But weeds have grown in the Garden of Eden. A quarter of British boys aged sixteen have sex with a fifth of similar girls, only half of them using contraceptives. Some girls happily seek childbirth, even to bring up the baby alone, because it means the instant prestige of adulthood. A third of the cases of gonorrhoea in British women occur under the age of nineteen. The blights of sex are overpopulation and disease, necessitating essential education in:

(a) the connection between copulation and conception;
(b) the connection between copulation and infection;
(c) whether children should be given free contraceptives once they are able to walk, thus reducing teenage pregnancies; or whether children should not be given free contraceptives until they are able to drive, thus increasing teenage morality. (A futile argument in practical education, which conceives in many adults a pleasant self-important pomposity.)

As repetition encourages absorption, the facts of (a) and (b) could be imparted briefly at every morning's school assembly. Religion having become an irrelevance to education, such practical instruction would produce a compensating improvement in the statistics of sin.

Most of the school sex class is preaching to the physically converted, young people generally gigglingly finding out about the fun from each other. My own sex education, in less head-shaking days, was fittingly delegated to the sports master. His springtime briefing in the cricket pav, among the bats and pads and the whiff of linseed oil, beginning: 'You have something between your legs, and sometimes it goes stiff', was to the relief of the prospective players shortly redirected to mysteries of the lbw Law.

Freud's Couch Potatoes

Psychiatry was invented in 1902 by the Psychological Wednesday Society, which met for coffee in the flat over the butcher's shop at 19 Berggasse, near the Danube Canal in north Vienna. After the meeting they played the undemanding card game tarot, but no drinks, because their host, Sigmund Freud, had a neurosis about the effect of even a small one on his thinking.

By 1908, they felt themselves important enough to become the Vienna Psychoanalytic Society, and by 1910 even more important, and became the International Psychoanalytic Association. These gatherings created psychiatric theories with the *élan* of chamois leaping up the Tirolean Alps. They never troubled over the tedious verification of their ideas, but elaborated them into exciting new ones, while joyfully mixing earthy medicine with airy philosophy. Perhaps it was all the effect of the strong Viennese coffee.

By 1913, Freud developed another neurosis about 'the human rabble' not appreciating these rarified doctrines after his death, and formed a secret circle of six psychological evangelists, among whom he distributed ancient Greek gold rings of deep psychological significance.

All his disciples were industriously psychoanalysing each other. This must have been a rewarding exercise, because they were a rum bunch. Dr Victor Tausk was good-looking, broke, a chronic depressive, enticed from his family by Lou Andreas-Salomé, a queenly woman given to fox-furs, eighteen years older than he was, a new pupil of Freud's and the impressive ex-mistress of Rilke the poet and Nietzsche the philosopher (both psychopaths). Freud himself took a fancy to her in 1912, sending her bouquets and chocolates and admiring her work, and going home with her late at night, declaring how curious it was that she presented to him no sexual attraction (how reassuring is human hypocrisy). She doubled as a useful spy on Tausk, Freud having developed a paranoid neurosis that Tausk was pinching his best psychoanalytical ideas.

Many females fell in love with Freud on his consulting couch, which he modestly ascribed not to his attractiveness but to his substitution for the truly loved one. He was then analysing the thirty-five-year-old analyst Helene Deutsch, making a spot diagnosis that she was after him sexually from her once forgetting her handbag on the famous couch. To solve the Lou Andreas-Salomé awkwardness, he referred analyst Tausk to Helene for analysis. Tausk was now divorced from his feminist wife, and decided to marry one of his own analysis patients who was sixteen years younger, to Freud's outrage. But on his wedding eve in 1919, Tausk committed suicide thoroughly by shooting himself while wearing a noose, so hanging himself as he dropped, after wisely drinking a bottle of slivovitz.

Another disciple, Herbert Silberer, had a row with Freud over the interpretation of dreams. Freud sent a two-line note saying he never wanted to see the man again. On a January night in 1923, Frau Silberer came home from a party, opened the front door and confronted Herbert's face, hanged, lit with a torch carefully arranged on the stairs. Freud refused also the presence of Sandor Ferenczi, who had decided that his patients desired a mother-substitute and kept kissing them, though he was dying of anaemia (he was such a hypochondriac that nobody knew). In 1911 Alfred Adler renounced the libido and formed a splinter group, in 1934 Carl Jung went home to Switzerland, and shortly afterwards Hitler arrived in Vienna and most of the psychoanalysts, being Jews, had other things to worry about.

From this incestuous intellectual hotbed emerged the infantile doctrine of Freud. This grew into a spoiled and misunderstood *enfant terrible*.

A handy rehash of Freud's ideas:

1   *The Libido*. Sex is the nuclear fuel of life, the driving force transmitted to power all our activities (Jung went home to Zurich to enlarge on this notion). We are unconscious of this lifelong power, we simply delight in the brilliance of its everyday effects, but if it explodes the fall-out is catastrophic.

2   *The Id*. This nasty little beast, which prowls dangerously in the deepest layers of our unconscious, embodies our basic instincts – to have sex, to be aggressive, and to survive in this world whatever the cost. The wants of the id must be immediately satisfied, and it knows of nothing but pain and pleasure. The *ego* is the keeper of the id, controlling the beast with (obviously) varying success. The prissy *superego* struggles to keep the ego up to the job, having learned that in human society there are some things that ids simply cannot do. The superego has enjoyed long-standing moral approbation as 'this Deity in my bosom', our conscience.

3   *The Oedipus Complex*. Every little boy is eager to have sex with mother, facilitated by his first killing father, who wishes to frustrate such plans by castrating him. Girls have the Electra

complex about father instead. This does not seem to bother most families.

4 *Dreams.* Our night's dreams feature our day's unsatisfied desires, all disguised like the dancers at an all-night fancy-dress ball. If we dream about anything pointed – umbrellas, rifles, pencils, snakes, fountains – it is a penis. If hollow – cupboards, cookers, churches – it is the vagina. Anxiety dreams of missing trains, and sudden nakedness in the bus, express sexual desires. Dreams may be fascinating to the dreamer, but over the cornflakes are utterly uninteresting. ('He tells me his stupid dreams every morning nearly,' meek Carrie was obliged to complain about Mr Pooter.) Freud scientifically proved this misbelief with his masterwork *The Interpretation of Dreams*, which was published in 1899 and took six years to sell 351 copies.

5 *Penis Envy.* The growing girl discovers from her brothers and boy playmates that she has not got one. This makes her puzzled, resentful and tediously difficult.

6 *Freudian Slips.* The expression of a repressed wish in a slip of the tongue. To psychoanalysts, anyway.

7 *Hysteria.* The escape into blameless illness from beleaguered health. Sufferers develop paralysis, pains, numbness, blindness, fits, amnesia or various grotesque symptoms without being ill, for some advantage and without entirely knowing what they are doing. Hysteria is Greek for womb, the condition originally being considered exclusively feminine (it was assessed in 1816 as due to lack of sexual pleasure), to be treated by removal of the clitoris. When Freud described hysteria in men, he met the incredulity and ridicule later invoked by women wishing to become priests.

8 *Thanatos.* The death instinct, expressed

individually by suicide, drink, drugs, smoking, ovcreating, underexercising and motorway pile-ups. Expressed nationally by the glory of war.

9 *Sadism and Masochism*. Until 1905, Freud thought this the extension of normal sexual union, the male dominant on top, the female submissive on the mattress. Feeling that he was flogging a dead horse, he promoted masochism to an expression of *thanatos* the death-wish, with the sadist kindly lending a helping hand. Everyone knows of the Marquis de Sade, who died mad in 1814. Leopold von Sacher-Masoch was an Austrian policeman's son, the author of *Venus in Furs*, who died in Prussia in 1895. He was furious at having masochism named after him by the Viennese psychiatrist Krafft Ebing, despite his liking for kissing the boots of the women in sables who were whipping him while he was dressed as their maid.

10 *Fetishism*. Settling for the symbol rather than the sexual. A male aberration, part of the castration complex – some men subconsciously fear that, on giving their penis to a female, they will not get it back. Fetishists can achieve orgasms only in macs and wellies, or when the woman is wearing their favoured shoes or rubber or leather outfits. Feel and smell have a powerful effect. Some men are attracted only by a specific bit of a woman, such as her eyes, legs or nipples. Some steal their fetishes, the stealing being part of the fun. One man needed six mackintoshes of different makes in bed with him to achieve an orgasm.

11 *Psychoanalysis*. This technique of psychotherapy, fashioned over coffee on Wednesday afternoons in Vienna, now chatters on busily across the world. Perhaps its comfort is no more than pouring out your heart to your friends and relations; but friends and relations

213

do seem to have so many other things to do, and other people's sorrows, like their dreams, are dreadfully boring.

Freud's ideas today, like Newton's, enjoy more reverence than relevance. Freud was a physician, at first a lecturer in neuropathology at the General Hospital in Vienna, who applied to the mind the scientific disciplines applied to the body. He tidied up the chains struck off madmen at the Bicêtre Hospital in Paris and Bedlam in London a century before. The paths of glory are littered with publicity handouts, and Freud's pen left three million words in his repute. He modestly claimed only to have disturbed the sleep of the world: awakening man saw himself in a distorting mirror, and is still unsure whether to take fright or burst into giggles.

How to Change Your Sex

Much unnecessary fuss has been made about, and by, homosexuals. Homosexuality is a simple and fairly harmless psychological aberration. Some homosexuals are created perhaps by their genes, or by their hormones: we are all male and female, painted not in stark sexual colours but in varying shades, some delicate. Some become homosexuals *faute de mieux* in schools, the Services, ships, prisons. Some are not homosexuals at all, but men and women who will cheerfully take a sexual shy at anything, or who flaunt homosexuality to curtain their sexual inadequacies and social insignificance, or to win themselves favours and advance their worthy careers. Some humans are too immature emotionally to grapple at a heterosexual union, and some men are simply scared flaccid of women.

When homosexuality caught Professor Kinsey's scientific eye, 37 per cent of the male population of the United States had tried it, and 4 per cent had continued doing it. The normality of such behaviour floats or sinks on the devious currents of public opinion. Sappho, the poetess with gay abandon from Lesbos, was the adored pivot of female literary society in the seventh century BC, as she would be today. Plato in the fourth century BC was having little boys and considered to be doing them the world of good. In 1895, Oscar Wilde was righteously sent to Reading Gaol; in 1974 the American Psychiatric Association was solemnly proclaiming homosexuality as non-pathological; and in between the Nazis were hounding homosexuals into concentration camps and damning them further with pink triangles on their hideous striped prison uniforms.

Male homosexuals are currently unpopular for transferring AIDS, because they insert their penis into the rectum, which has a delicate and absorbent lining (before the perfection of intravenous drips it was used to infuse fluids, chemicals and nourishment into the body), instead of into the vagina, which has a lining similar to, and as tough as, the skin on her nose. Animals are freely homosexual, and many lovely butterflies are genetically one sex and physically the other.

Transvestism is a form of fetishism which affords sexual gratification to some homosexuals. Their desire to be female may be so strong that they try pushing their penises into their body, but transvestites want to change their clothes rather than their sex. The next step is transsexualism, 'gender dysphoria', an overwhelming restlessness with your own sex and an impregnable conviction, in defiance of your chromosomes, that you are a member of the other one.

Unlike homosexuals, who prefer sex with their own sex *as* their own sex, transsexuals want it with the other sex. They develop a harrowing obsession to alter

215

their sex anatomically. This occurs in one in 50,000 people, and is proof against psychiatric or pharmacological treatment.

The condition was first explored by the Greek satirist Lucian in the second century. In his *Conversations in the Underworld*, the skeleton of the philosopher Menippus greets that of the soothsayer Tiresias as the only person in the living world who had been both male and female. Menippus inquires, which condition was enjoyed most? Oh, it was much more fun being a woman, Tiresias replies: there is so much less to do, no soldiering, no jury service, no tedious public meetings, and women can always boss their husbands about. But what about the agonies of childbirth? asks Menippus sympathetically, inquiring if he had ever had a baby. Tiresias admits no, though adding sharply that he had a perfectly good vagina. Menippus does not believe him, any more than that Daphne was turned into a laurel tree.

Since the famous creation of Christine Jorgensen in 1951, the science of surgery has made this credible.

Changing a Man into a Woman

1 *Providing a vagina.* The first requirement.
   Gynaecologists have ample experience of this
   operation, because the vagina may be
   congenitally incomplete or absent – just a
   dimple in the skin between the urethra and the
   anus. In women, the procedure to restore the
   defect dissects out a vagina in the loose tissue
   between the bladder and the rectum. Performed
   de novo in men, it is more awkward because of
   the narrower, non-child-bearing pelvis, and the
   prostate getting in the way. The operation was
   improved by Sir Archibald McIndoe, the plastic
   surgeon of the RAF 'Guinea-pigs' with smashed
   faces in World War Two. Sir Archibald took

tissue-paper-thin skin grafts, which he otherwise applied to faces, to line the new vagina, inserted round a mould like a generous penis. As these grafts contract over the years, other surgeons prefer the full-thickness skin graft with its underlying nourishing tissue, or a transplant of bowel, but this drips mucus.

2 *The penis.* This is filleted of its spongy erectile tissue. The penile nerves are preserved, and the penile skin used for the vaginal opening, or it may be stretched to line the vagina. The urethra running along the penis, through which the man passes urine, is partly retained and replaced in the female position in the new genitalia.

3 *The testes.* Removed. The scrotum becomes the new labia majora – the sensitive lips surrounding the opening of the vagina.

4 *Optional extras.* The male breasts can be enlarged with plastic implants. The nose and the ears are easily reduced in size, operations by themselves favoured in transsexuals who are wary of going the whole sow. The give-away male Adam's apple can be reduced to female shape by surgery of its cartilages. Sexually superfluous hair is removed by electrolysis.

Changing a Woman into a Man

1 *Creating a penis* More awkward than excavating a vagina. The shape of the organ is difficult to reproduce; the urethra, which ends in front of the vaginal opening, must somehow be elongated to its tip, and the surgeons face the erection problem. A pedicel of skin can be raised on the abdominal wall and later transferred to the clitoris region, or skin grafted from the forearm and linked to the pudendal nerve in the pelvis to provide sex stimulation. A silicone stiffener can be applied for insertion into the mate's vagina. Orgasms are achievable with this arrangement. The designer penis may be startlingly hairy from

the transferred skin, though its looks can be improved by a circular skin graft creating a glans at the end. Penile construction has been sufficiently successful for the demand for female-to-male change to catch up with the male-to-female. An alternative is enlarging the clitoris with hormones then bolstering it with skin-flaps, but it is not much use for purposeful entry into a vagina.

2 *Obliterating femininity*. The uterus and ovaries are excised and the vagina constricted or removed.

3 *The Testes*. Prostheses shaped like testicles are suspended in a scrotum made from the drawn-down skin of the labia on each side of the vaginal opening.

4 *The Breasts*. Removed. Some women so hate their breasts that they flatten their chests with tight bindings to pretend that they do not exist.

Such ingenious plastic surgery is not assayed as freely as removing wrinkles and double chins. The patient must first be treated with hormones and scanned by psychiatrists, and spend a transvestite year living in the new gender. Whether it is all worthwhile, or not entirely worth the bother, is not as beautifully plain as the results of commonplace plastic surgery. Transsexuals who have felt of, and lived as, the other sex since childhood are better with the difficult sexual and social postoperative adjustment. Sometimes resentment strikes, the new men and women returning to their former clothes, jobs and beings, and seeking reversal of their complex surgery – which is irreversible. Sufficient cases of transsexualism benefit, in the eyes of its surgical enthusiasts, to warrant its continuance. But what is the cause of the condition? Nobody knows.

Humans escaping from God's simple function of the sexual urge – to produce more men and women – may feel resentful at being studied so zealously by scientists. Or they may be comforted that their departure from rigid normality is no more condemnable than developing a peptic ulcer or any other statistically scrutinised condition. Science only observes, measures, correlates, foresees. It is neither mystical nor arrogant, but humble towards its known, and its infinite unknown, limitations.

The novelist and playwright Somerset Maugham qualified as a doctor at St Thomas's Hospital in London in 1897. Medicine was then becoming familiar with microbes and antiseptics and anaesthetics and X-rays, and discarding its witch's robes of the early nineteenth century for the scientific mantle. Maugham recalled in 1938 from the sunlit reposefulness of Cap Ferrat this encouraging scientific homily:

> I remember that once in the Dissecting Room when I was going over my 'part' with the Demonstrator, he asked me what some nerve was and I did not know. He told me; whereupon I remonstrated, for it was in the wrong place. Nevertheless he insisted that it was the nerve I had been in vain looking for. I complained of the abnormality and he, smiling, said that in anatomy it was the normal that was uncommon. I was only annoyed at the time, but the remark sank into my mind and since then it has been forced upon me that it was true of man as well as of anatomy. The normal is what you find but rarely. The normal is an ideal.

THIRTEEN

Seeing The Joke

....

Man is the only creature endowed with the power of
laughter. Is he not also the only one that deserves to be
laughed at?

Caption to a Rowlandson cartoon, 1802

To speak truly, he is not to me a good companion, for most
of his conceits were either scripture jests, or lascivious
jests; for which I count no man witty: for the devil will help
a man, that way inclined, to the first; and his own corrupt
nature, which he always carries with him, to the latter.

Izaak Walton, *The Compleat Angler*

....

The Unalarming History of Sexual Humour

The fault of Sigmund Freud's *Wit and its Relation to the Unconscious* is its author taking a sledgehammer to crack a joke. Its painstakingly analytic relationship to wit and humour is comparable to Gray's *Anatomy* opened alongside a girlie magazine. Its unchallengeable inclusion among the world's unfunniest books is achieved by 162 indexed jokes: like the one Freud got from Heine, about the chiropodist who found himself sitting next to Baron Rothschild, 'and he treated me quite as his equal – quite famillionairely'. Freud spends the next six pages examining this line, with diagrams, ending up with people 'falling into their anecdotage' and

'Christmas being the alcoholidays', but missing the point of a gentle dig in silk-waistcoated ribs.

Another of Freud's jokes:

> A regular customer enters a Viennese pastry-cook's and orders a cake. He shortly returns, requests a glass of Tokay instead, downs it, and leaves without paying. The pastry-cook remonstrates. The customer says: 'But I gave you the cake back.' 'But you didn't pay for the cake, either.' 'Yes, but I hadn't eaten it.' (This necessitates six pages of explanation.)

Another, with Freud's help for those missing the point:

> 'A horse-dealer was recommending a saddle-horse to a customer. "If you take this horse and get on it at four in the morning you'll be at Pressburg by half-past six." – "What should I be doing in Pressburg at half-past six in the morning?" '
> Here the displacement leaps to the eye. The dealer obviously mentions the early hour of arriving at the provincial town simply in order to demonstrate the horse's capacity by an example. The customer disregards the animal's capacity, which he does not question, and merely enters into the data of the example that has been chosen. The reduction of this joke is accordingly easy to give.

Which recalls the Bruce Bairnsfather cartoon of World War One, showing a fed-up old soldier leaning against a shattered brick wall with a chatty young one asking: 'Who made that 'ole?' 'Mice,' the other tells him. The Germans, having decided that Tommy's sense of humour was vital for morale, tried to install a similar one in their own troops. They reproduced this drawing in a manual on humour, adding helpfully: 'It was not mice. It was a shell.'

Another: 'How beautifully Nature has arranged it that as soon as a child comes into the world it finds a mother ready to take care of it!' Not too bad.

Another: 'A doctor, as he came away from a lady's bedside, said to her husband with a shake of his head: "I don't like her looks." "I've not liked her looks for a long time," the husband hastened to agree.'

Twenty-six years later, two men meet in a Frank Reynolds cartoon in *Punch*:

> 'Where are you off to?'
> 'To the doctor. I don't like the look of my wife.'
> 'I'll come with you. I hate the sight of mine.'

Freud published *Wit and its Relation to the Unconscious* in 1905, because he had finished *The Interpretation of Dreams* and was seriously puzzled that our dreams should contain jokes. He wrote the new book synchronously with *The Theory of Sexuality*, the two manuscripts lying on adjoining tables in his study at No. 19 Berggasse in Vienna, adding to either according to his mood of the moment. It is thus understandable that *Wit and its Relation to the Unconscious* should contain sexy jokes, like:

> 'Mr and Mrs X live in fairly grand style. Some people think that the husband has earned a lot and so has been able to lay by a bit; others think that the wife has lain back a bit and so has been able to earn a lot.'
>
> A really diabolically ingenious joke! and achieved with such an economy of means! 'Earned a lot – lay by a bit; lain back a bit – earned a lot.' It is merely the inversion of these two phrases that

distinguishes what is said about the husband from
what is hinted about the wife.

Freud conceived that the jokes which we all tell are –
like everything else that we do, from mass murder to
slips of the tongue – produced by our subconscious mechanism. As I mentioned, this consists, roughly, of the
superego nervously supervising the *ego*, which is con-
tinually struggling to control the filthy, wild, sex-mad
id, in the unlit basement of our mind which houses the
power cables and fuse-box.

Freud was specific about sex jokes told by men in front
of women: 'The smutty joke is like a denudation of a
person of the opposite sex toward whom the joke is
directed. Through the utterance of obscene words, the
person attacked is forced to picture the parts of the body
in question, or the sexual act, and is shown that the
aggressor himself pictures the same thing.'

So when I offer a woman a medical Joe Miller like:

FEMALE PATIENT TO HER DOCTOR: 'Kiss me, darling.'
DOCTOR: 'Kiss you? My God! If I kissed you I'd get
in the most *awful* trouble! The General Medical
Council! Struck off the *Register!* Lose my
livelihood! (*Reflects a moment.*) As a matter of fact,
I shouldn't really be in bed with you at all.'

I am then unthinkingly performing the equivalent of an
obscene phone call, if not rape. If her husband is present,
I am accused by Freud of committing verbal adultery.
Her only defence of her virtue is to look lost and say that
she doesn't understand it. (Mr Gladstone, resuscitator of
fallen women, was unable to understand any joke whatever with a sexual reference.)

Even if I considerately direct my dirty joke to another
chap, 'the woman is exposed before the third person,
who now as a listener is bribed by the easy gratification

of his own libido'. How disgusting of me! Better stick chastely to mothers-in-law and Irishmen. Though as Freud observed shrewdly: 'Women give vent to or appreciate humour so much more rarely than men.'

Sexy Chestnuts

The sniggerers' Bible is Gershon Legman's 1969 *Rationale of the Dirty Joke*, which was thirty years in the writing and contains 811 pages of conscientious analysis of two thousand examples of crude humour. These vary from anecdotes rambling along to a wildly swiping punch-line, to two-liners from a box of dirty Christmas crackers.

The stories have three characteristics: (1) They are much the same. (2) They are not new. (3) They are not particularly funny.

> The bellboy is accused of having raped the chambermaid by catching her with her head out of the window watching a parade, locking her head there by pulling down the window, and having intercourse with her from behind. 'Why didn't you call for help?' asks the judge. 'Well, Judge, I didn't want people to think I was cheering for a Republican parade.'

The compiler comments:

> The situation of being locked in place erotically by a window-blind also occurs in *Tristram Shandy*, while Casanova describes a real incident of exciting himself and a woman by watching a public execution from a window overlooking the scene, and having intercourse with the woman from behind while she is gobbling up the scene optically, leaning out of the window.

This captive sexual position was used in 1348 by Boccaccio in *The Decameron*, to form the second story of the seventh day.

Peronella of Naples, a poor mason's wife, takes in her gallant every morning and locks the front door once her husband has left to seek work. One morning, he surprises them by banging on the door shortly afterwards. Peronella directs in panic: 'I am a dead woman, for lo, here is my husband, foul fall him! . . . for the love of God, be it as it may, get thee into this tun that thou seest here, and I will open to him, and we shall see what is the occasion of this sudden return.'

She shrewishly castigates her husband for his coming home workless: 'What are we to live on? whence shall we get bread to eat? Thinkest thou I will let thee pawn my gown and other bits of clothes? Day and night I do nought else but spin, insomuch as the flesh is fallen away from my nails, that at least I may have oil enough to keep our lamp alight . . . Other women have a good time with their lovers, and never a one have we here but has two or three; they take their pleasure, and make their husbands believe that the moon is the sun; and I, alas! for that I am an honest woman, and have no such casual amours, I suffer, and am hard bested: I know not why I provide not myself with one of these lovers, as others do.'

The husband interrupts proudly: 'I have found means to provide us with bread for more than a month; for I have sold to this gentleman, whom thou seest with me, the tun, thou wottest of, seeing that it has encumbered the house so long, and he will give me five gigliats for it.' She replies that she has just sold it for seven gigliats to a man who is inside, inspecting it. The gallant leaps out, complaining that the tun is encrusted with lees. 'My husband will scour it clean,' Peronella assures him.

The husband is scraping away inside in a trice; Peronella directs operations, her head stuck through the vent of the tun; her gallant, as 'the wild and lusty horses do amorously assail the mares of Parthia, he sated his youthful appetite'. He had the decency to pay the seven gigliats, but he got the husband to carry the tun to his house.

Boccaccio lifted the story lock, cock and barrel from Lucius Apuleius's *Golden Asse*, which was written in Latin twelve hundred years earlier. The vixenish wife protests her innocence, and complains of her poverty. She says, in the 1566 translation: 'I poore wretch doe nothing day and night but occupie my self with spinning, and yet my travell will scarce find the Candels which we spend. O how much more happy is my neighbour Daphne, that eateth and drinketh at her pleasure, and passeth the time with her amorous lovers according to her desire.'

The only difference from Boccaccio's version is Apuleius's couple copulating inside the tub, while the husband is underneath cleaning its bottom. 'This minion lover cast his wife on the bottome of the tub and had his pleasure with her over his head, and as he was in the middest of his pastime, hee turned his head on this side and that side, finding fault with this and with that, till as they had both ended their businesse, when as he delivered seaven pence for the tub, and caused the good man himselfe to carry it on his backe again to his Inne.'

Moral: There is no such thing as a new joke.

A similar predicament arose later in New York:

> A pregnant young woman asks the doctor what position she will have to lie in to give birth to the baby. 'The same position you were in when you started it.' 'My God,' she exclaims, 'do you mean

I've got to drive around Central Park in a taxi for
two hours with my feet hanging out the window?'

Gershon Legman perceives: 'The bride is clearly compet-
ing with the doctor-father, in the matter of mockery ...
but it is equally clear that his superior status is carrying
the victory.'

Rude words are a complication within rude jokes. If I
say: 'Duck!' everyone ducks; but if I say: 'Fuck!' everyone
recoils in outrage. The reason today is obscure, when we
discuss both these bodily contortions with equal open-
ness. But our taboos are powerful, and are nervously
self-imposed by awareness of our overwhelming sexual
desires.

There's the one about the schoolteacher whose train
stopped in the wild west, with a solitary Red Indian on
the platform:

> 'Are you a real Indian?' 'Ugh.' 'How many wives do
> you have?' 'Eight.' 'But what do you do with so
> many wives?' 'Fuckum.' 'Why, you dog!' 'Fuckum
> dog too.' 'But my dear!' 'No can fuckum deer. Deer
> run too fast.'

To lose the Indian's verb loses the point. Similarly with
a story I heard in an Australian hospital:

> A novice Tibetan monk approaches the lama
> superior with the terrible confession that he has an
> overpowering desire to perform sexual intercourse.
> The lama is wonderfully understanding: 'My boy,
> we wisely make provision for such natural youthful
> desires here in the monastery.' The novice says:
> 'Oh, good.' The lama directs: 'Descend to the
> basement, where you will find hanging on the wall
> a golden key. Insert it in the stout door straight
> ahead, and you will discover inside the stable of
> an extremely well-kept female yak, upon whom you

may bestow your exuberant love.' The novice descends, finds the key, opens the door, and returns all smiles. The lama asks: 'I hope that afterwards you thanked the yak? That you patted it and soothed it, and offered it a lump of sugar?' The novice shuffles his feet and confesses: 'Er, no.' The lama is furious. 'You young people nowadays are all the same! It's always a case of fuck you, yak, I'm all right!

A story popular after World War Two featured a gallant Polish fighter-pilot who had flown with the RAF:

The hero is invited to present the prizes at his local girls' school. An inevitable question from the girls afterwards is: 'Tell us, wing commander, how did you win your VC?' 'It was very easy,' he explains gutturally and modestly. 'I was up in my Spitfire, when I saw that Fokker ahead of me, so I shot the Fokker down. Then I saw another Fokker below me, so I shot the Fokker down. There was another Fokker on my tail, but I dived, and I shot the Fokker down.' The headmistress, listening with rising agitation, exclaims: 'Er, wing commander, perhaps you would explain to the girls that the Fokker was a type of German aeroplane?' 'Oh, yes,' he agrees. 'But these Fokkers were Messerschmitts.'

Substituting the anatomical or physiological terms for everyday ones ruins erotic jokes and literature. To transcribe a common scene in a modern novel:

Her respiration rate rose rapidly as she felt her Bartholin glands lubricating the vestibular area in anticipation of intercourse. She groped across the sheet for his erect penis, which she took by the glans, lightly flicking the external urinary meatus with her thumbnail. (The clitoris was erect also.) He was meanwhile digitally palpating her anal sphincter, initiating its reflex contraction, while applying lingual stimulation to the areola, including the glands of Montgomery, surrounding her erect nipples. As she abducted her femora, he inserted the phallus between the labia majora, continuing internally between the labia minora into the vaginal orifice. He reached the vault of the vagina, and after some minutes' coition ejaculated from his seminal vesicles 5 ml of sperm, with a normal count of 80×10^6, into the posterior fornix in the region of her cervix. She experienced contraction of the levatores ani muscles of the pelvis as she simultaneously underwent orgasm. She inhaled deeply, and said: 'Whatever would my husband think?'

The literary effect is admittedly lost.

D. H. Lawrence in *Lady Chatterley's Lover* conscientiously and repeatedly refers to the gamekeeper's phallus. If he misspells it with an 'o', he was an inexcusably careless writer, who muddles the uterus with the vagina. Lawrence suffered also a restricted knowledge of sexual physiology:

> It was obvious in them too that love had gone through them: that is, the physical experience. It is curious what a subtle but unmistakable transmutation it makes, both in the body of men and women: the woman more blooming, more subtly rounded, her young angularities softened, and her expression either anxious or triumphant: the man much quieter, more inward, the very shapes of his shoulders and his buttocks less assertive, more hesitant.

This is rubbish. Lawrence had no sense of humour, either. He would never have enjoyed cracking a dirty joke, even seriously with Freud.

Indecent jokes do not exist for doctors. As bodily functions are their bread and butter, they become instead workplace funny stories.

Example from 1820: 'I say, doctor, could you tell me why my wife should have a little one, and we've only been married six months!' 'Oh, yes, it often happens with the first but never afterwards.'

To the layman, these can sound heartless:

'What's the smallest pub in the country?'
'The Thalidomide Arms.'

Exam question. Early Parkinsonism is diagnosed by
a characteristic rhythmical movement of the
thumbs upon the forefingers. What would you
advise an actor who developed it? *Answer.* To get
a part in a commercial for roll-your-own cigarettes.

A country GP gravely informed the local young
nobility in the springtime that their five-year-old
heir with leukaemia had but six months to live.
Time passed. Christmas came. The bedridden
patient still lingered. The couple plainly expressed
doubts on the doctor's all-round abilities. One
afternoon, they discovered him on his knees beside
the bed. They overheard his prayer: 'Die, you little
bugger, die!'

When a medical student at Bart's I anthologised a few awful jokes, which enjoy a curious indestructibility among the students today.

On a church outing to the seaside, two middle-aged
men get out to pee behind a hedge. Unfortunately,
the coach reverses, exposing them indecently.
Afterwards, one of them apologises, all flustered,
to his wife, who says: 'Oh, but I was so proud when
you got *ours* out!'

The wife is expressing a subconscious sublimation of penis envy, invented by Freud in 1923. When a little girl discovers that she lacks a penis she transfers her love to her father, but mixed with envy, because he commands something which she has not, apart from the family car.

A man swallows his glass eye. He is sent to hospital, where the ophthalmologist refers him to the gastronterologist, who inserts a long, old-fashioned metal sigmoidoscope into his anus, and goes on inserting it, as if drilling a tunnel. 'Well, I can't see anything,' the doctor confesses. 'That's funny,' remarks the patient, who is lying on the couch with legs drawn up, facing the opposite way. 'I can see *you*.'

All such jokes about inserting things into bodily orifices compensate for the inescapable, but worthy, humility this procedure inflicts on the medical profession.

A man goes to his doctor saying he wants to lose weight. The doctor prescribes tablets, directing: 'Take one on retiring.' That night, the patient dreams that he is alone on a desert island. Then from behind a rock appears a fierce cannibal, with a chopper. He chases the patient all over the island, luckily not catching him, but after all that exercise he wakes in the morning having lost five kilos. Another man goes to the same doctor with the same request, receives the same prescription, and that night dreams that he is alone on a desert island. A delicious native girl appears naked from behind a rock. The patient chases her all over the island, unluckily not catching her, but after all the exercise by morning has lost five kilos. After several exhausting nights these two patients get together – patients somehow always do. The first returns to the doctor in anger: 'Why am I chased all night by a dirty great cannibal, when the other patient

spends his nights chasing a beautiful nude
woman? I demand an explanation!' The doctor says:
'Oh, that's simple. Your fellow-slimmer is one of
my private patients. But you, poor sod, are NHS.'

This illustrates that doctors are indifferent to sexual, but
not to financial, discrimination.

Did you hear about the two Eskimos who got
engaged? One cold night they broke it off.

And the girl who married a Pole? She had a check-
up first.

Did you read that bit in the obstetrical journal? 'She
underwent an orgasm in a non-coital situation.'
All the author meant was: 'She came unscrewed.'

What do girls put behind their ears to please men?
Their knees.

'How do you get dandruff off a cunt?' (*The man
asked shakes his head. You vigorously brush his
shoulder.*)

'How do you get rid of superfluous pubic hair?' (*You
stick out your lower lip and go: 'Pppphhhhtttt!'*)

Necrophilia is dead boring.

These jokes demonstrate (however regrettably) that even
scientists have an ability to lark about with the English
language.
   'Dad, I've got engaged.' 'Good on you, son.' 'And she's
a virgin.' 'Then you can forget it. If she's not good enough
for her own family, she's not good enough for ours.' This
incest joke is traditional in the island of Tasmania, where
the families of convicts released from Port Arthur offered
a restricted choice of partners, and where they cheerfully
bear such incestuous stigmata as twelve fingers (which
must be useful for playing Schönberg).

Two businessmen are leaving after a weekend at a colleague's charming country place. One says warmly to their host through the car window: 'Thanks a lot, old man! Delightful house, lovely food and drink, and your wife makes a bloody good screw.' As they drive off, his companion mentions: 'Wasn't that a rather odd thing to tell him?' 'Oh, yes,' the other agrees. 'But one must be polite. Actually, she was a bloody awful screw.'

A man drives up to a country pub, and produces a handful of coins for his drink, including two pink plastic golf-tees. 'What are they?' asks the young barmaid curiously. 'Oh, they're what I rest my balls on when I drive.' She sighs: 'Ask a silly question, get a silly answer.'

In the chuffing days of the Flying Scotsman, the steward Albert faithfully served the travelling railway bosses with their meals for years. When he retires, they decide to present so devoted a railway servant, and a man who always strictly obeyed regulations, with an old dining-car parked on a disused siding in some lovely Scottish glen, to pass his time before hitting the buffers of life. When the directors some years later are travelling in Scotland, they say: 'Let's look old Albert up! Let's see how he's been enjoying the terminus years in a clapped-out diner.' But as they approach the siding, they are horrified to see frail Albert between the buffers, slowly pushing the dining-car along the track. They run to help, crying in alarm: 'What's the matter?' Albert replies: 'Nothing sir, but the old woman's on the lavatory.'

A duck staying in a luxury hotel in Hong Kong has a woman in his room. He phones down to room-service for a condom. The Chinese floor-waiter knocks, with the condom on a silver platter, and the duck says: 'Put it on my bill.'

These four stories prove only that anyone who laughs at them has an admirably sensitive sense of humour.

Doctors' comic stories are mostly told against their own profession, which already enjoys the healthy mockery of the patients. I have shamelessly enjoyed the idle and undisciplined life of a writer by doing little else. 'Novelists are lucky to get paid anything,' accurately perceived Beryl Bainbridge, 'scribbling away and expecting to be thought terribly important for it.'

The reason that medicine makes such estimable comic copy is:

> The objects of wit are institutions or their agents, moral or religious precepts that command so much respect that they can be approached in no other way than by jokes.

Freud said so, but perhaps he was joking.

FOURTEEN

The Sexual Apocalypse

....

The sexual impulse is a force, to some extent an incalculable
force, and the struggle of the man to direct that force, when
he and it are both constantly changing, is inevitably attended
with peril, even when the impulse is normal or at all events
seeking to be normal.

Havelock Ellis, *Psychology of Sex*

....

A Cautionary Fable

God was walking in the garden of Eden in the cool of
the day. Hands clasped behind the waist of his purple
mantle, long curly golden beard bowed low on his chest,
deep in thought he paced sedately across a velvety lawn
which sprouted snowy edelweiss, sunny primroses and
dusky orchids, wandered into a glade of coconut palms,
oaks, firs and giant cacti, sat on a cedar log and picked a
banana.

There was a whirring noise, and the Angel Gabriel
fluttered up.

'Hello! Haven't seen you for aeons,' God greeted him
in surprise.

'I was being angelic on Planet Earth.' Gabriel folded
his wings and sat on a toadstool.

'And how are my ratings down there?'

'Bad,' said Gabriel.

God's brow expressed displeasure.

'I've flown round churches of all sorts, and apart from the spectaculars the audiences are pretty terrible.' Gabriel was honest to God. 'Though I must say, I look rather nice in stained glass.'

'Very different from the eighteenth century, even the nineteenth,' God observed sombrely. 'It's my own fault. Since I let mankind into the secrets of science, they no longer have the flattering belief that I run everything personally, and so they had to keep on the right side of me. What's the point in performing miracles, when they can all be explained away by chemical reactions and reproduced in some smelly lab? Nowadays they listen to those men in white coats, not my men in surplices.'

'They've become frightfully religious about their environment. They worship the air and the trees.'

'The heaven and the earth which I created, instead of me myself? I told you, humans are a materialistic lot.'

Gabriel shrugged his wings. 'But they have to revere *something*, you know. Even the most conceited of them need an anchor in the sky.'

God grunted and extended his hand, which was instantly occupied with an onyx beaker, to be filled by a cherub with nectar. 'Have a drink,' he invited more jovially.

Gabriel shook his long blonde curls. 'Couldn't face another. On earth, they're at something or other bottled all day long.'

God guffawed. 'All Noah's fault. He should never have planted a vineyard as soon as he got out of the Ark.'

'The Côte d'Ararat was quite drinkable,' said Gabriel knowledgeably, flicking the edge of his white linen robe across his ankles.

'Then have a Jordan water.' God snapped his fingers, and a crystal goblet was sparkling in the angel's hand.

'I'm rather peckish,' he confessed, as a golden dish of dazzling white sandwiches appeared on the log.

'That manna looks different,' Gabriel observed curiously.

'Yes, I'm creating it ready-sliced,' God told him proudly. 'It's the greatest thing.'

'I'm worried about Earth's destiny,' imparted Gabriel, reaching for a tasty sandwich of smoked dragon's wing. 'You should never have given humans free will, you know.'

'I didn't,' God reminded him gruffly, taking a sandwich of devil's kidney. 'I created man, and he grew into free will without my expecting it.' He indicated the bees busy round his sandwich. 'Just like these insects grew the ability to make honcy.'

'On earth, those bees can give you a nasty sting.'

'Really? My earthly creatures *do* seem to have developed a propensity to be unpleasant to each other. Perhaps they enjoy it.'

'The motor car has made them even ruder,' Gabriel told him feelingly. 'That time you sent me down to Nazareth, everyone knelt in the streets. Now they hoot at me. They think I'm publicising something.'

'The motor car is an invention of the Devil! Do you know, some imp was up here last Christmas, tempting me with a new model chariot of fire? What was I talking about? Ah, yes, free will. I had a word with that philosopher fellow – what's his name, like the chappie who scores all those runs on the Elysian Fields – '

'Hobbes.'

'That's it. But all these philosophers are impossible,' God broke off wrathfully. 'Why, they think they know more about eternity than I do.'

'*Reductio ad absurdum*,' murmured Gabriel reverently.

'Oh, *nescio quid mihi magis farcimentum esset*,' God brushed it aside.

An eagle, a dove and an ostrich appeared at a respectful distance, looking hungrily at the sandwiches. A lion and a polar-bear padded tamely by.

'What's gone wrong with the human being?' God demanded, reaching for the roast unicorn. 'I gave him a decent brain.'

'That's the trouble. In today's world, only the brainy ones earn the take-home talents.'

'Then how do the dimmer lot get their daily bread?' asked God in concern.

'They take to sin, mostly.'

'Dear me,' said God sombrely. 'And of course, men fight, which I never intended. You must have read in my book that "Greater love hath no man than this, that a man lay down his life for his friends"?' Gabriel nodded obediently. 'But as I told Horace perfectly plainly, he took the idea far too dangerously with his *"dulce et decorum est pro patria mori"*, not to mention Homer in Greek, which escapes me for the moment.'

'They usually laid down their lives for ambitious and unscrupulous politicians,' observed Gabriel sadly. 'But perhaps they liked the excitement. Though I must say, they do seem to be getting out of the habit.'

' "Peace, perfect peace, in this dark world of sin",' God hummed. 'Wrote a good hymn, did the Reverend Bickersteth. Yes, but that's only because I allowed them a peep into the secrets of nuclear physics. With these fancy new bombs, the troublemakers are scared stiff of being blown to pieces themselves. That's the only way to stop mankind misbehaving, you know. Terror. The Black Death was a great idea, it crammed the churches. They're quite as faint-hearted as Hamath and Arpad at Damascus. You read about them in my book?'

'But you know mankind's greatest disaster?' Gabriel

informed him. 'The sexual urge which you bestowed upon them.'

God looked amazed. 'That was to be unalloyed pleasure, to ensure their multiplication.'

'It has caused as much division as multiplication. They go forth and multiply with one partner, fine. Then they fancy another, and go forth with them. Makes for a lot of squabbling. Mind, the lawyers do well out of it.'

'I wouldn't know,' God admitted. 'I never meet one up here.'

'Sex urges them into all sorts of odd performances. Men with men, women with women. No multiplication in that. It can get really dangerous – fiddling about with children, rape, even murder.' God winced. 'And weird practices, like tying themselves up with ropes, and advertising their specious charms in *Private Eye*. They even take videos of themselves doing it.' God held a hand over his eyes. 'Besides exploiting sex quite ruthlessly for selling things.'

'What sort of things?'

'Soapy things, mostly.'

'Isn't the Church doing its job?' God asked sternly.

'The Church is only concerned with chastity. Which is like curing bellyache by telling everyone to stop eating.'

'I was rather afraid of this sort of thing happening,' God recalled resignedly. ' "Variety's the very spice of life" – so that gloomy fellow Bill Cowper tells me. Trouble is, a lot of mankind nowadays want more spice than life. Perhaps I'd better get rid of them all?' he suggested abruptly. 'They're an ungrateful lot of buggers.'

Gabriel nodded his halo vigorously in agreement.

'It's easily done,' God continued with relish. 'You know, the seven angels with the seven golden vials full of the wrath of God. It's all in my book. Plenty of action in Revelation.'

'I think that would be unnecessarily painful,' Gabriel objected.

'I could explode the Earth? Or hit it with Jupiter. I rather enjoy playing astronomy.'

'Don't do that. It looks so pretty spinning round in the sky.'

God had a divine inspiration. 'Tell you what! I'll simply cancel this sex urge, and mankind will stop reproducing. Come a century, they'll all have died off naturally, and nobody will have felt an unnecessary twinge.'

'Not a bad idea,' said Gabriel thoughtfully. 'They've got another century just coming up. It would be neat.'

'Exactly. From midnight on 31 December 1999, no human being will have any sexual interest whatever in any other.' God snapped his fingers again, smiling broadly. 'It's done. So simple, so effective. Solve everybody's troubles. Yes, an excellent idea!' He playfully turned the angel's Jordan water into wine.

'A lot of New Year parties are going to end rather lamely,' Gabriel reflected with a sigh. 'I do hope that you're going to leave them sex on television? They've got to have *something* to do in the evenings.'

Bibliography

....

IN THE BEGINNING
Thurber, J. and White, E. B., *Is sex necessary?* London: Hamilton, 1929

VIRGIN TERRITORY
Frazer, Sir J. G., *The golden bough* (2nd ed.), London: Macmillan, 1950
Huizinga, J., *The waning of the middle ages*, London: Arnold, 1924
Stone, L., *The family, sex and marriage in England 1500–1800* (2nd ed.), Harmondsworth: Penguin, 1979
Maurois, M., *The bedside esquire*, London: Heinemann, 1941

OUR ROYAL VIRGIN
Feiling, K., *A history of England*, London: Macmillan, 1950
Hibbert, C., *The virgin queen*, London: Penguin, 1992
Strachey, G. L., *Elizabeth & Essex*, London: Chatto, 1932

A SEXUAL EMPIRE
Johnson, C. (ps Defoe, D.), *Histoire des pirates anglais*, Paris: L'editions français illustrée, 1921
Ballhatchet, K. *Race, sex and class under the Raj*, London: Weidenfeld, 1980
Feiling, K., *A history of England*, London: Macmillan, 1950
Huizinga, J., *The waning of the middle ages*, London: Arnold, 1924

Hyam, R., *Empire and sexuality*, Manchester: University Press, 1990

Stanford, J. K., *Ladies in the sun*, London: Galley Press, 1962

SWEETHEARTS AND WIVES

Cronin, V., *Napoleon*, London: Collins, 1971

Fraser, Sir W., Bt, *Hic et ubique*, London: Samson Low, 1893

Gordon, R., *Great medical mysteries*, London: Hutchinson, 1984

Herold, J. C., *Mistress to an age*, London: Hamilton, 1959

Jameson, E., *The natural history of quackery*, London: Joseph, 1961

Masson, F., *Napoléon et les femmes* (10th ed.), Paris: Ollendorff, 1894

Masson, F. (ed.), *Napoléon inconnu: papiers inédits 1786–1793*, Paris: Ollendorff, 1895

Pocock, T., *Horatio Nelson*, Oxford: Bodley Head, 1987

Sladen, D. (ed.), *Lord Nelson's letters to Lady Hamilton*, London: Library Press, 1905

Wilson, H., *Memoirs* (vol. 2), London: Navarre Soc., 1924

A SOUND OF REVELRY BY NIGHT

Bushell, T. A., *Imperial Chislehurst*, Chesham: Barracuda, 1974

Herrick, C. T. (ed.), *The letters of the Duke of Wellington to Miss J. 1834–1851*, London: Fisher Unwin, 1924

Longford, E., *Wellington: the years of the sword*, London: Weidenfeld, 1969

Thompson, N., *Wellington after Waterloo*, London: Routledge, 1986

Villiers, G., *A vanished Victorian*, London: Eyre & Spottiswode, 1938

VICTORIAN VALUES

Blake, R., *Disraeli*, London: Eyre & Spottiswode, 1967

Longford, E., *Victoria R. I.*, London: Weidenfeld, 1964

Pearsall, R., *The worm in the bud*, London: Weidenfeld & Nicolson, 1969

Reid, M., *Ask Sir James*, London: Hodder, 1987

Sheppard, F., *London 1808–1870*, London: Secker & Warburg, 1971
Wright, L., *Clean and decent*, London: Routledge, 1960

VICTORIAN VAGARIES
Comfort, A., *The anxiety makers*, London: Nelson, 1967
Knight, S., *Jack the ripper*, London: Harrap, 1976
Marcus, S., *The other Victorians*, London: Weidenfeld & Nicolson, 1966
Odell, R., *Jack the ripper*, London: Harrap, 1965
Pearson, M., *The age of consent*, Newton Abbot: David & Charles, 1972
Trudgill, E., *Madonnas and magdalens*, London: Heinemann, 1976

THE MYTH OF FEMINISM
Fulford, R., *Votes for women*, London: Faber, 1957
Laver, J., *Clothes*, London: Burke, 1952
Mill, J. S., *The subjection of women* (ed. Coit, S.), London: Longmans, 1906
Riencourt, A. de, *Sex and power in history*, New York: McKay, 1974
Rubinstein, D., *Before the suffragettes*, Brighton: Harvester Press, 1986
Smith, H. L. (ed.), *British feminism in the twentieth century*, Aldershot: Elgar, 1990
Taylor, A. J. P., *English history 1914–1945*, Oxford: Clarendon, 1965

SEX HEIL!
Bezymenski, L., *The death of Adolf Hitler*, London: Joseph, 1968
Bleuel, H. P., *Strength through joy*, London: Secker & Warburg, 1973
Bullock, A., *Hitler, a study in tyranny*, London: Odhams, 1952
Grunberger, R., *A social history of the third Reich*, London: Weidenfeld & Nicolson, 1971
Heiden, K., *Der Fuehrer*, London: Gollancz, 1944
Heston, L. and Heston, R., *The medical casebook of Adolf Hitler*, London: Kimber, 1979

Meissner, H-O., *Magda Goebbels*, London: Sidgwick & Jackson, 1980
Shirer, W. L., *The rise and fall of the Third Reich*, London: Secker & Warburg, 1960
Speer, A., *Inside the third Reich*, London: Weidenfeld, 1970

SEXUAL ODDITIES
British Medical Journal, 1979, i: 1163–4
Enoch, M. D. and Trethowan, W. H., *Uncommon psychiatric syndromes* (2nd ed.), Bristol: Wright, 1979
Frazer, J. G., *The golden bough* (2nd ed.), London: Macmillan, 1950
The Times, 24 February 1994
World Medicine, 14 January 1976: 44–7
World Medicine, 22 January 1983: 24–5

THE SEXUAL SCIENTIFIC REVOLUTION
British Journal of Hospital Medicine (vol. 41), January 1989, 15–16
Kinsey, A. C., Pomeroy, W. B., Martin, C. E., *Sexual behavior in the human male*, Philadelphia: Saunders, 1948
McCarthy, J. (ed.), *Plastic surgery* (vol. 6), Philadelphia: Saunders, 1990
Roazen, P., *Freud and his followers*, London: Lane, 1976

SEEING THE JOKE
Freud, S., *Jokes and their relation to the unconscious*, London: Hogarth Press, 1960
Legman, G., *Rationale of the dirty joke*, London: Cape, 1969